LEGO Disney

Character Guide

Written by Simon Hugo

Contents

Walt Disney

"We're just getting started"

THIS IS THE MAN who started it all. A master storyteller with an eye for character, Walt set up his animation studio and co-created Mickey Mouse while still in his twenties. He went on to make some of the world's best-loved movies, and his magical world is still going strong more than 100 years later!

CAMERA MAN

Walt's minifigure is part of a realistic movie camera set celebrating 100 years of Disney animation. Opening the camera reveals a drafter's desk for Walt.

Did you know?

Walt Disney set up his animation studio with his brother Roy on October 16, 1923.

Need to know

Likes: Family, stories, innovation
Dislikes: Waste, repeating himself
LEGO® debut (shown here): 43230 Walt Disney Tribute Camera (2023)

Oswald the Lucky Rabbit

Hops and dreams

THIS BUSY BUNNY needs all the luck he can get! His big ideas get him into all kinds of trouble, but somehow good fortune always gets him out of it again. There's no job he can't make more interesting with his sense of mischief and invention—plus his elastic, endlessly detachable body parts!

EARLY ICONS
Oswald is one of four screen icons to get the stylized LEGO® BrickHeadz™ treatment in Disney 100th Celebration (40622), alongside Mickey Mouse, Snow White, and Tinker Bell.

Need to know

Likes: Adventure, second chances
Dislikes: Obeying the laws of physics
LEGO debut: 40622 Disney 100th Celebration (2023)
Minifigure shown: 71038 Disney 100 Series (2023)

Did you know?

Making his screen debut way back in 1927, Oswald is officially Disney's first cartoon star!

Mickey Mouse

Join his club

THE WORLD'S MOST FAMOUS mouse is a happy-go-lucky adventurer with a heart of gold. He is a friend to everyone, but his can-do spirit and infectious positivity sometimes get him and his pals into hot water! Luckily, Mickey is also a quick thinker and can be counted on to save the day with a smile.

Need to know

Likes: Minnie Mouse, whistling
Dislikes: Being mistaken for a rat
LEGO debut: 4164 Mickey's Fire Engine (2000)
Minifigure shown: 71040 Disney Castle (2016)

Head and ears make an iconic three-circle silhouette

Smart suit to welcome Disney Park visitors

Fabric LEGO coattails piece

Red pants with white buttons

MAGIC OF MICKEY
A huge, brick-built Mickey wearing his sorcerer's apprentice garb from 1940's *Fantasia* stands tall in the 2024 LEGO® Ideas set Magic of Disney (21352).

Full steam ahead

This monochrome minifigure (40659) recreates Mickey's very first look, from the 1928 black-and-white cartoon short *Steamboat Willie*.

Medieval mouse

As a brave knight, Mickey wears gleaming armor and a unique head piece with a built-in silver helmet (10780).

Minnie Mouse

Take a bow ...

THE WORLD'S SECOND most famous mouse doesn't begrudge Mickey his icon status. She knows he loves the spotlight! Minnie is more focused on making sure everyone around her is happy, and she will do all she can to help people achieve their dreams. She is kind to everyone but has no time for bullies or bad behavior.

Need to know

Likes: Mickey Mouse, gardening
Dislikes: Fighting, rudeness
LEGO debut: 4165 Minnie's Birthday Party (2000)
Minifigure shown: 71040 Disney Castle (2016)

MAXI MINNIE
The classic Minnie model in Mickey Mouse & Minnie Mouse Buildable Characters (43179) is based on her appearance in the 1930s and stands around 14 in (36 cm) tall.

Firehouse mouse
Minnie and Mickey wear matching red uniforms as minifigure firefighters (10776), though Minnie accessorizes hers with a bow!

Paw substitute
Minnie swaps polka dots for paw prints and a molded skirt for a fabric one in 2025's Minnie's Pet Hotel (43274).

Donald Duck

Fowl tempered

HE MAY GREET every day with a smile, but this duck's temper cracks like an egg! The slightest setback sends him into a feathery fury. His girlfriend, Daisy, and his three beloved nephews do their best to calm him down, but they can't help finding his tantrums very, very funny!

Need to know

Likes: Daisy Duck, Huey, Dewey, and Louie
Dislikes: Setbacks, looking foolish
LEGO debut: 71012 Disney Series 1 (2016)
Minifigure shown: 71040 Disney Castle (2016)

Down on the farm

Donald wears a plaid shirt with an ear of wheat in his pocket in 2021's Mickey Mouse & Donald Duck's Farm (10775).

Quack a joke

Donald is cast as the court jester with a unique head piece in the 2022 set Mickey and Friends Castle Defenders (10780).

DUCK TAILS
Both Daisy and Donald come with a special duck tail piece designed to slot in between a minifigure's legs and torso.

Daisy Duck

Feathered fashionista

THIS SOPHISTICATED STYLE ICON prides herself on her grown-up ways. She is skilled at defusing Donald's temper tantrums and prefers the finer things in life over action and adventure. But that doesn't stop Daisy from being playful, enthusiastic, and fun-loving—and occasionally unleashing a temper of her own!

EPIC WELCOME

Daisy, Donald, Minnie, and Mickey all stand ready to meet and greet guests in the Disney Castle (71040), an epic 4,080-piece set from 2016.

Duck to water

Daisy wears a swimsuit with a fabric skirt for a seaside visit to Minnie Mouse's Ice Cream Shop (10773) from 2021.

Bygone Daisy

Queen Daisy swaps her bow for a crown when she steps back in time for some olden-days fun with jester Donald.

Need to know

Likes: Donald Duck, fashion
Dislikes: Losing her temper
LEGO debut: 71012 Disney Series 1 (2016)
Minifigure shown: 71040 Disney Castle (2016)

Goofy

Simple soul

GOOD OLD GOOFY may be clumsy and easily confused, but he more than makes up for it with his big heart and willingness to laugh off his troubles. Most of the time, he is blissfully unaware that he even has troubles, which can cause headaches for Mickey, Minnie, Donald, and Daisy. But they always forgive their lovable friend.

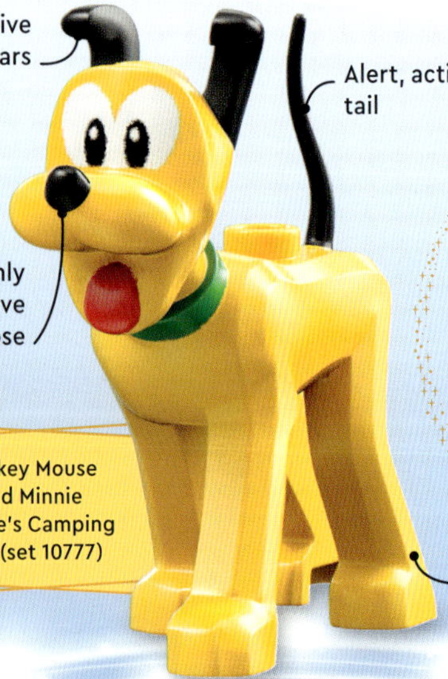

Did you know?

Mickey, Minnie, Donald, Daisy, Goofy, and Pluto are collectively known as Disney's "Sensational Six."

THIS CLUED-IN CANINE is Mickey Mouse's best pal, pet, and confidant. He lives the life of a happy hound: doing tricks, eating treats, and generally sniffing out adventure. Pluto likes to chase cats—and sometimes chipmunks, too—but he means them no harm. Really, he just wants to be loved by all.

Pluto

Mickey's mutt

Chip 'n Dale

Nuts about nuts

Need to know

Likes: Nuts, trees, mischief
Dislikes: Getting on each other's nerves
LEGO debut (shown here): 71024 Disney Series 2 (2019)

THIS CHEEKY CHIPMUNK PAIR adore acorns and other nuts and will do anything to stock up on them! Chip is the bossy brains of the operation, and accident-prone Dale is ... also present. Their single-minded mission causes plenty of trouble for Mickey Mouse, Donald Duck, and Pluto—and for themselves, of course!

Did you know?

Chip 'n Dale play smartly dressed train conductors in 2019's motorized Disney Train and Station set (71044).

GUMSHOE GEAR
In LEGO BrickHeadz form, Chip 'n Dale (40550) wear their cool crime-fighting outfits from the *Rescue Rangers* TV series.

Scrooge McDuck

Richest duck in the world!

DONALD DUCK'S UNCLE has so much money, he can literally swim in it. His riches are the result of two things: hard work and doing his best to never spend a dime! Once, he loved his wealth more than anything else, but now he puts his family first—especially his grandnephews Huey, Dewey, and Louie.

Scrooge McDuck, Huey, Dewey, and Louie:
Disney Series 2
(set 71024)

Huey, Dewey, and Louie

Triple trouble

AS JUNIOR WOODCHUCK SCOUTS, these identical triplets are quick-thinking, determined, and resourceful. They put these skills to good use on globe-trotting treasure hunts with their great-uncle Scrooge McDuck—and to less-good use playing pranks on their uncle Donald. The adult ducks rely on the boys' color-coded clothes to tell the trio apart!

Snow White

Friend to all

Did you know?

Snow White and the Seven Dwarfs was the first ever full-length Disney movie, and Snow White is the original Disney Princess.

THIS KIND, GENTLE princess is loved by everyone except her wicked stepmother, the Evil Queen. When the Evil Queen's jealousy forces Snow White to flee their castle, she finds a new, much happier home in the woods with seven new friends. The Evil Queen tries to end her once and for all, but true love saves the day.

Need to know

Likes: Animals, singing, helping others
Dislikes: Getting lost in the woods
LEGO debut: 10738 Snow White's Forest Cottage (2017)
Mini doll shown: 43205 Ultimate Adventure Castle (2022)

Snow alternative

Snow White's minifigure is found in two sets (43222 and 43242) and comes with a choice of two faces: one smiling and the other sleeping peacefully.

The Seven

Snow White's forest family

WHEN SNOW WHITE leaves home to escape her wicked stepmother, she takes refuge in a secluded woodland cottage. It is home to seven hard-working jewel miners who welcome her into their little world. When the disguised Evil Queen comes calling at their hidden home, the steadfast seven bring her evil reign to an end.

Happy

Smiles are guaranteed with the most social member of the seven—who is also the most likely to break out into song!

Bashful

Shy even when Snow White isn't around, Bashful can usually be found giggling into his beard when she is in sight!

All characters:
Snow White and the Seven Dwarfs' Cottage (set 43242)

Sleepy

Digging for jewels all day would make anyone exhausted, but no one feels it more than poor old Sleepy!

Grumpy

The moodiest member of the team has a permanent scowl, but beneath his grouchy exterior, he has a heart of gold.

Doc

The self-proclaimed leader of the seven is kindly and wise, even if he's a little bit pompous and prone to mix up his words!

Sneezy

Hay fever has Sneezy in its grip, but he doesn't let it stop him from playing his part in cottage life.

Dopey

The youngest member of the group never speaks, but his playful nature leaves no doubt about his cheery outlook.

Did you know?

Dopey's alternative LEGO face has a lip print on the forehead, where he was kissed by Snow White.

The Prince

Singing his heart out

SNOW WHITE'S TRUE LOVE is captivated by her singing voice before he first sets eyes on her. He scales high walls to join her in song, but their courtship is cut short when Snow White has to flee the family castle. He searches far and wide to find her again, and their eventual reunion saves her life.

Did you know?

Neither "the Prince" in *Snow White* nor "Prince Charming" in *Cinderella* are given proper names in their animated films.

Need to know

Likes: Singing, romance
Dislikes: Losing Snow White
LEGO debut: 43222 Disney Castle (2023)
Minifigure shown: 43242 Snow White and the Seven Dwarfs' Cottage (2024)

FULL HOUSE
The Prince is one of 10 minifigures in Snow White and the Seven Dwarfs' Cottage (43242), plus some of Snow White's animal friends.

The Evil Queen

Vain and vicious

SNOW WHITE'S STEPMOTHER has little time for her royal duties. She is far too busy obsessing over her looks and gazing into her Magic Mirror. When the mirror says that Snow White is more beautiful than she is, the Evil Queen sets out to get rid of her stepdaughter entirely—first with brute force, then with a poisoned apple!

Need to know

Likes: Being told she is beautiful
Dislikes: Snow White, true love
LEGO debut: 71038 Disney 100 Series (2023)
Mini doll shown: 43276 Snow White's Jewelry Box (2024)

MIRROR, MIRROR ...
The Evil Queen can consult her Magic Mirror—with ghostly mini doll-style reflection—in the Snow White's Jewelry Box set (43276).

Royal robes

The Evil Queen's collectible Minifigure (71038) wears a fabric cape and comes with a Magic Mirror accessory.

Dark disguise

A very different minifigure (43242) shows the Evil Queen in disguise when she sets out to trick Snow White with a poisoned apple.

Pinocchio

No strings attached

BROUGHT TO LIFE by the Blue Fairy, this puppet won't become a real boy until he proves himself brave, selfless, and truthful. He sets out to do just that but is led astray by dreams of stardom and the temptations of Pleasure Island. It takes a great act of heroism to get him back on track.

Did you know?

In *Aladdin*, the Genie makes his face look like Pinocchio when he thinks Aladdin is lying!

ON THE NOSE
LEGO Pinocchio's nose doesn't change size, but it is still something of a novelty. Most minifigures have no nose at all!

Need to know

Likes: Singing, dancing
Dislikes: Turning into a donkey
LEGO debut (shown here): 71038 Disney 100 Series (2023)

Geppetto

Caring carver

Did you know?

Geppetto features alongside the likes of Belle, Lilo, and Simba in the LEGO Ideas set Magic of Disney (21352).

THIS MASTER CARVER brings joy to children with the wooden toys he makes, but he longs to be a father with a child of his own. He pours all his love into a puppet named Pinocchio, then wishes on a star for his creation to come to life. The Blue Fairy hears him and grants his wish!

PINOCCHIO'S BEST FRIEND is a tiny little insect appointed by the Blue Fairy to be the wooden boy's official conscience. He helps Pinocchio learn the difference between right and wrong and sticks with him when things get tough. Jiminy is far from perfect, though, and his adventures with Pinocchio teach him a few things, too.

Jiminy Cricket

Little voice worth listening to

Dumbo

Extraordinary elephant

THERE'S NO OTHER elephant like this one. Dumbo uses his ears to fly! At first, he thought he needed a magic feather, but then he learned he could do it all by himself. Dumbo's first LEGO appearance came in 2023, in the same set as Bambi and a special Walt Disney minifigure.

Dumbo and Bambi: Walt Disney Tribute Camera (set 43230)

Bambi

Everyone's favorite fawn

Did you know?

Dumbo was first seen on screen in 1941. Bambi made his movie debut just one year later.

ONE DAY, THIS YOUNG deer will grow up to be the Great Prince of the Forest, keeping other woodland animals safe from danger. But for now, he is a young fawn learning how to walk, talk, and thrive through the changing seasons. Bambi appears in just one LEGO set, which was released to celebrate 100 years of Disney films.

Cinderella

Shall go to the ball

WITH HER ANIMAL FRIENDS and optimistic nature, Cinderella makes the most of life as an overworked servant in her own family home. When she meets her fairy godmother, she enjoys a magical night at a royal ball—and ends up being freed from her cruel stepmother and two selfish stepsisters once and for all.

Need to know

Likes: Animals, dancing
Dislikes: Rudeness, snobbery
LEGO debut: 41053 Cinderella's Dream Carriage (2014)
Mini doll shown: 43266 Cinderella's Dress (2025)

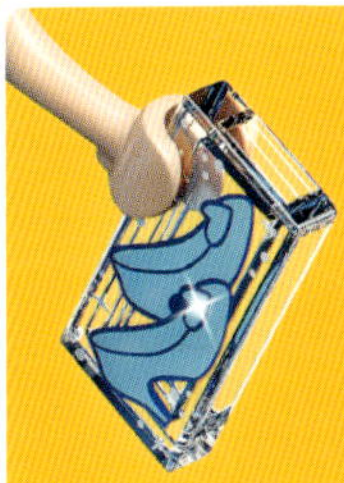

IF THE SHOE FITS ...
Cinderella's famous glass slippers are represented by a printed LEGO tile in Cinderella's Royal Carriage (43192) from 2021.

Mix and match

Four princesses, including Cinderella, can choose whether to wear skirts or pants in 2024's Disney Princess Market Adventure (43246).

Elegant accessories

Cinderella wears a crown, an elegant gown, and long evening gloves in Princess Enchanted Journey (43216) from 2023.

Hair to the throne

The Cinderella minifigure from 2023's Disney Castle (43222) is the first to wear this hair and headband piece.

Fairy Godmother

All good in a hood

CINDERELLA'S SENSE OF HOPE is strong—so strong that it conjures up her fairy godmother! This kindly figure appears out of nowhere when Cinderella is at her lowest and gives her the strength to carry on. With a few magic words, she gives Cinderella the one chance she needs to change her life forever.

Did you know?

The fairy godmother sometimes forgets her own magic words, "Bibbidi-bobbidi-boo!"

Need to know

Likes: Dreams coming true
Dislikes: Losing her magic wand
LEGO debut: 41146 Cinderella's Enchanted Evening (2017)
Mini doll shown: 43192 Cinderella's Royal Carriage (2021)

FROM SQUASH TO POSH
Cinderella's Royal Carriage (43192) includes a LEGO pumpkin piece and the majestic coach that the fairy godmother turns it into.

Prince Charming

Having a ball

Did you know?

Prince Charming appears as a dashing minifigure alongside Cinderella in 2023's Disney Castle (43222).

Cinderella's Castle & Horse Carriage (set 43275)

THIS REBELLIOUS ROYAL resists all calls for him to get married—until he meets Cinderella! At a ball attended by families from across the kingdom, she's the only one who grabs his attention, and they quickly fall in love. When Cinderella is forced to flee without giving her name, the prince makes it his mission to find her again.

Cinderella & Prince Charming's Castle (set 43206)

CINDERELLA'S FATHER DIED when she was very young, leaving her in the care of her stepmother, Lady Tremaine. She favors her two spoiled daughters over the gentle Cinderella, who works as their servant. Lady Tremaine is obsessed with seeing her offspring do well, but she has raised them to be mean, vain, and lazy.

Lady Tremaine

Severe stepmom

Cinderella's Animal Friends

And one animal adversary!

CINDERELLA SHOWS GREAT kindness to the mice that visit her home and to her pet dog, Bruno. She tries her best with Lucifer the cat, but he simply won't be won over! When Cinderella's fairy godmother transforms the friendly creatures for a night at the royal ball, grumpy Lucifer gets left out of the magic.

Bruno

Cinderella grew up with this loyal, loving bloodhound, who becomes a smartly dressed human footman for her trip to the ball.

Cinderella's Castle Celebration (set 43178)

Lucifer

Lady Tremaine's mean-spirited cat enjoys getting Bruno into trouble, tormenting Cinderella, and trying to eat her mouse friends!

Lucifer and Gus: Cinderella's Castle & Horse Carriage (set 43275)

Gus

This brave mouse is devoted to Cinderella. When she goes to the ball, he pulls her carriage as a magically transformed white horse!

Alice

Adventurer in Wonderland

Did you know?

Alice in Wonderland is based on an English children's story written more than 160 years ago!

LONGING FOR A more unusual life, this determined young dreamer takes a trip down a rabbit hole and finds herself in Wonderland. Here, she meets curious characters who talk in riddles and creatures that never knowingly make sense. The more Alice explores their strange world, the more she appreciates her everyday existence!

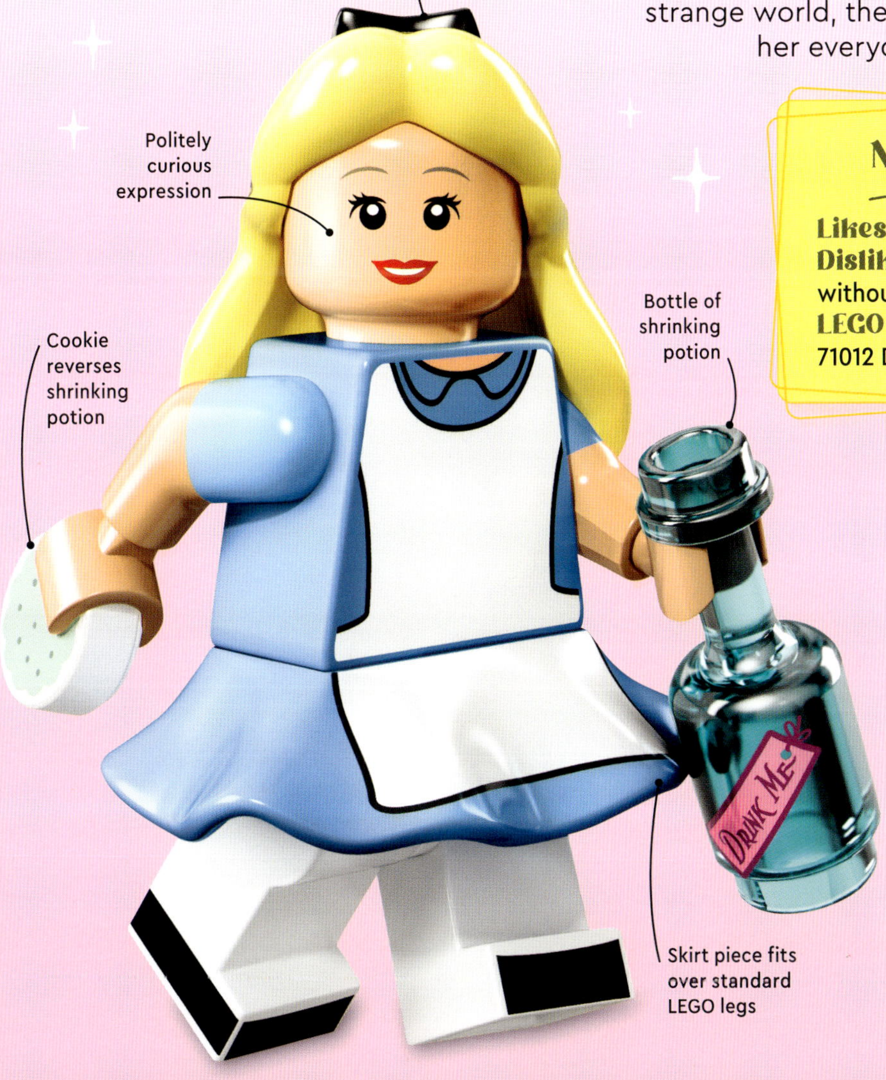

Need to know

Likes: Daydreams, cats
Dislikes: Rudeness, books without pictures
LEGO debut (shown here): 71012 Disney Series 1 (2016)

Dress to impress

Alice transformed into a mini doll for her appearance in 2023's The Enchanted Treehouse (43215), complete with detailed patterns on her white pinafore.

Queen of Hearts

Maniacal monarch

THE SUPREME RULER of Wonderland is just as irrational as her realm! Straight out of a pack of cards, she enjoys playing games—especially croquet—but her favorite thing is losing her temper. The Queen loves striking fear into her timid subjects and is shocked when Alice tires of her tyrannical tantrums!

Did you know?

When the Queen of Hearts plays croquet, she uses a flamingo as a mallet and a hedgehog as a ball!

Disney 100 Series (set 71038)

The Cheshire Cat

Perplexing puss

Disney Series 1 (set 71012)

THIS CURIOUS KITTY is the closest thing Alice has to a guide in Wonderland. The first sign he is about to appear is a huge grin hanging in thin air. Then, when he disappears, his eyes and smile are the last thing to leave! Alice looks to the Cheshire Cat for advice, but his tricks also get her into trouble.

Peter Pan

Never grows old

Lost in a book

This micro doll Peter appears in a storybook-style set inspired by the 2023 live-action Disney movie *Peter Pan & Wendy*.

LIFE IS A GAME for the leader of the ragtag Lost Boys. He has decided to never grow up and spends his days in Never Land, playing, flying, and getting into scrapes with pirates. He is confident to the point of carelessness, and the only time he is ever serious is when his friends are in danger.

Need to know

Likes: Adventure, stories
Dislikes: Losing his shadow
LEGO debut: 71012 Disney Series 1 (2016)
Minifigure shown: 43232 Peter Pan & Wendy's Flight Over London (2023)

SKY-HIGH SCENE

A microscale landscape makes the minifigures look like they are high above the city in Peter Pan & Wendy's Flight Over London (43232).

Tinker Bell

Foremost fairy

SHE MAY BE SMALL, but this fiery fairy is positively glowing with supersized power. She is much stronger than she looks, can mend almost anything, and can make anyone or anything fly with her pixie dust. She cares deeply for Peter Pan and needs all her magic and moxie to keep him out of danger!

Need to know

Likes: Peter Pan, fixing things
Dislikes: Pirates, banishment
LEGO debut: 71040 Disney Castle (2016)
Minifigure shown: 43212 Disney Celebration Train (2023)

Starting bell

The first Tinker Bell minifigure has smaller wings and a fabric skirt and wields a transparent green magic wand.

Mini doll debut

Tink became a mini doll in 2023, wearing all-new wings with detailed printing in The Enchanted Treehouse (43215).

MAGICAL MASCOT

Tinker Bell has long been a Disney mascot and joins in the 100th birthday fun in Disney Celebration Train (43212).

Wendy Darling

Living the dream

Did you know?

Micro dolls of Wendy and Hook as seen in the film *Peter Pan and Wendy* appear in one 2023 set.

YOUNG WENDY LOVES telling bedtime stories about Peter Pan and is delighted to learn that he's real. She dreams of staying young like him, but their adventures together in Never Land give her the confidence to keep on growing up. Getting older, she realizes, doesn't have to mean giving up on fun and imagination.

THE PIRATE CAPTAIN of the *Jolly Roger* is pursued by a crocodile everywhere he goes—and he blames Peter Pan! Getting revenge is his life's obsession, and he will never leave Never Land until Peter walks the plank or worse. To succeed, this beleaguered buccaneer will stop at nothing, from trickery to time bombs!

Captain Hook

Hung up on Peter Pan

Aurora

On course for a curse

ON HER SIXTEENTH birthday, Aurora learns she is a princess and that the aunts who raised her in a secluded wood are really three good fairies! For years, they've kept her safe from a curse, but she cannot escape its wicked magic forever. Only one thing can truly set Aurora free, and that is belief in true love.

Rise and shine

The princess wears a bell-shaped dress decorated with golden roses in Aurora's Royal Carriage (43173) from 2020.

By any other name

Roses reappear on this dress from Aurora's Forest Cottage (43188), echoing Aurora's childhood name, Briar Rose.

100 winks

In the Disney 100 Series (71038), Aurora's head piece can show a wide-awake face or a peaceful, sleeping one.

Need to know

Likes: Music, nature, Prince Phillip
Dislikes: Being treated like a child
LEGO debut: 41060 Sleeping Beauty's Royal Bedroom (2015)
Mini doll shown: 43240 Maleficent's Dragon Form and Aurora's Castle (2024)

Prince Phillip

Love's royal champion

WHEN PHILLIP AND Aurora meet, they instantly fall in love. Neither realizes the other is from a royal family—they are far too busy dancing to care! The brave prince proves his devotion when Aurora is struck by an evil fairy's curse. He fearlessly battles the fairy's dragon form to break her despicable spell.

ONE OF THE three good fairies who raised Aurora, Merryweather has been around the princess since she was a baby. She was there when an evil fairy put a curse on the child and acted quickly to change it with her own magic. The spell was not lifted, but Merryweather stopped it from being much worse!

Did you know?

So far, Merryweather is the only one of the three good fairies to be made into a LEGO figure.

Merryweather

Enchanted aunt

Maleficent

Fearsome fairy

THIS WICKED FAIRY wasn't invited to bless Aurora as a baby, so she chose to curse her instead. She revels in her villainy and strikes fear into everyone she meets, even the three good fairies. Her dark magic lets her fly, appear and disappear at will, and even turn into an enormous, fire-breathing dragon!

Need to know

Likes: Vengeance, misery
Dislikes: Kindness, heroism
LEGO debut: 71012 Disney Series 1 (2016)
Mini doll shown: 43240 Maleficent's Dragon Form and Aurora's Castle (2024)

DRAGON FAIRY
In her brick-build dragon form, Maleficent stands four times taller than a mini doll.

Icon of evil

This minifigure Maleficent wears a high fabric collar and a wicked grin in the Disney 100 set Villain Icons (43227).

The Raven

Diabolical bird

MALEFICENT'S CLOSEST COMPANION is a cruel yet capable raven. The wicked fairy rarely goes anywhere without the bird and relies on him to do her dreadful bidding. It is he who finds Aurora living happily with the three good fairies, just in time for Maleficent to fulfill her promised curse on the girl's sixteenth birthday.

PRINCE PHILLIP'S HORSE is strong and faithful—energized by oats and willing to go the extra mile for a bonus bag of carrots! When Maleficent takes Phillip prisoner, she makes sure to snare his steed as well. In their final battle against the evil fairy, Samson proves to be just as brave as his royal rider.

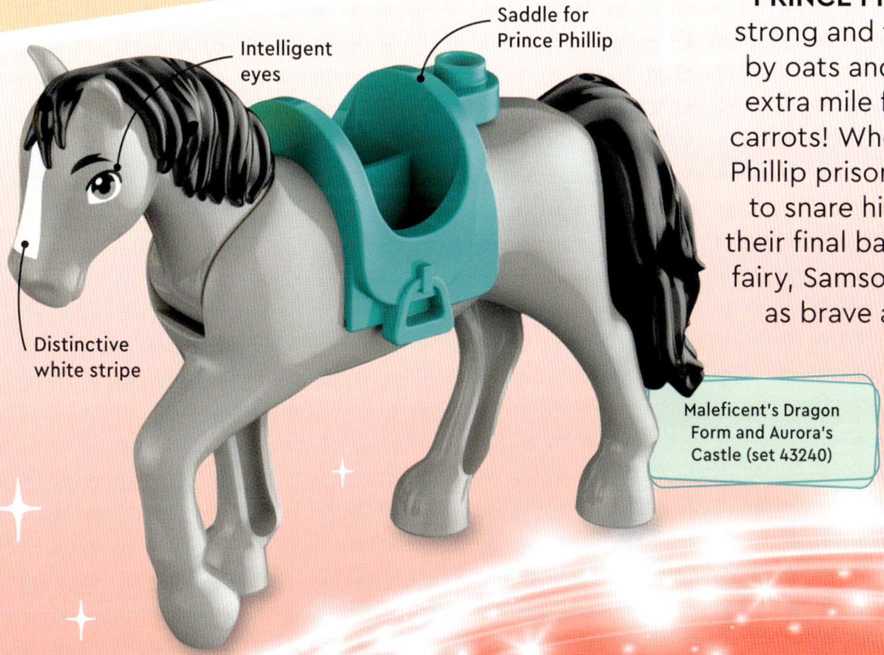

Samson

Heroic horse

The Dalmatians

Cuteness 101

THESE ADORABLE PUPPIES are just two among dozens held captive by Cruella De Vil. Fifteen are the offspring of devoted Dalmatian couple Pongo and Perdita, while another 84 are pet-store pups looking for their forever home. When they escape Cruella's clutches, they make one very big and happy family!

Spotted!

This minifigure-scale Dalmatian accompanies Cruella De Vil's collectible Minifigure from the Disney 100 Series (71038).

Did you know?

The 101 Dalmatians Puppy (43269) can be customized to make dozens of different Dalmatians (but not all at once)!

LUCKY, PENNY
Two more posable pups star in Lucky & Penny 101 Dalmatians Puppies (43271), complete with bone and TV builds.

Need to know

Likes: Playing, barking, food
Dislikes: Cruella De Vil
LEGO debut: 71038 Disney 100 Series (2023)
Figures shown: 43269 101 Dalmatians Puppy (2025)

Cruella De Vil

Fiendish fashionista

NOTHING MEANS MORE to this vain villain than looking like a million dollars. If that's bad news for the 101 Dalmatians, Cruella really doesn't care! With her mind on the catwalk and her eyes on the dogs, she will go to any lengths to impound more puppies in pursuit of her designer dreams.

Need to know

Likes: Clothes, fashion
Dislikes: Not getting her way
LEGO debut: 40620 BrickHeadz Cruella & Maleficent (2023)
Mini doll shown: 43262 Maleficent's and Cruella De Vil's Dresses (2025)

DRIVEN TO EXTREMES
Cruella De Vil's Car (43277) is a 2025 set featuring a Cruella minifigure, a Dalmatian figure, and one seriously evil-looking auto!

Disney 100 (and 1)

The Cruella that comes in the Disney 100 Series (71038) is literally two-faced and clutches a foxtail purse.

Winnie the Pooh

Silly old bear!

POOH BEAR SPENDS his days in the Hundred-Acre Wood, eating honey, having adventures with his friends, and thinking in his Thoughtful Spot. Despite his reputation as a bear of very little brain, he has a vivid imagination and is always on the lookout for Heffalumps, Woozles, and other extraordinary creatures!

Did you know?

Pooh and his friends were the first-ever LEGO® Disney figures, in LEGO® DUPLO® sets from 1999.

Need to know

Likes: Honey, balloons
Dislikes: Long words, bees
LEGO debut: 2981 Pooh and his Honeypot (1999)
Minifigure shown: 21326 Winnie the Pooh (2021)

HOME SWEET HOME
A corner of the Hundred-Acre Wood is recreated in the Winnie the Pooh set (21326), which opens to reveal a detailed interior.

Piglet

Pooh's number two

Did you know?

Both Tigger and Piglet star in their own movies—*The Tigger Movie* and *Piglet's Big Movie*!

Piglet and Tigger: Winnie the Pooh (set 21326)

POOH'S BEST FRIEND is nervy by nature but works hard to conquer his fears—which include heights, Heffalumps, and Halloween! He is very small but has a big impact in the Hundred-Acre Wood, doing kind and thoughtful deeds wherever he goes. When his friends need his help, Piglet never lets them down.

THERE'S NO ONE quite like Tigger—as he likes to remind his friends! He bounces through life in a blur of energy, leaving a trail of mishaps and mayhem behind him. But life in the Hundred-Acre Wood is all the more fun for his spring-loaded shenanigans, and his pals wouldn't have him any other way.

Tigger

Let's bounce!

Rabbit

Creature of habit

GIVEN THE CHOICE, Rabbit would rather be gardening than going on adventures. He likes things to be neat, tidy, and over by teatime. However, he feels a sense of duty toward his friends and rarely lets them get into trouble without him. Sometimes, he even adds his own trouble to the mix!

One-of-a-kind rabbit head piece

Indulgent smile

Carrot grown in Rabbit's garden

Rabbit and Eeyore: Winnie the Pooh (set 21326)

Did you know?

Eeyore wears a bow to make his tail easier to find when it falls off—which it does a lot!

Dejectedly droopy ears

Stitching holds Eeyore's sawdust in

Figure is all one piece, except for bow

EVEN MORE RELUCTANT than Rabbit, Eeyore goes along with Pooh's plans because it's too much effort to object. Deep down, the doleful donkey quite likes being gloomy, but he can't admit it because then the gloom would lift! His friends love him for his different outlook, and he loves them for not making him change.

Eeyore

Hundred-Acre mood

Marie

Parisienne puss

THIS PAMPERED PUSSYCAT lives in Paris with her mom, two brothers, and their rich owner, Madame Bonfamille. Madame adores her pets, but her greedy butler, Edgar, does not. When he ditches them far from home, Marie and her feline family must learn some street smarts to get back to Paris and expose Edgar's villainous schemes.

Did you know?

Marie can be seen in the 1996 version of *101 Dalmatians*, when the puppies watch *The Aristocats* on TV.

Need to know

Likes: Romance, singing, jazz music
Dislikes: Not getting her way
LEGO debut (shown here): 43286 The Aristocats Adorable Marie (2026)

CHIC CAT
Stylish Marie is never without a big pink bow around her neck. For this LEGO model, it is made from a unique fabric piece.

Robin Hood

Fox on the run

NOTTINGHAM'S NUMBER ONE OUTLAW is a wily fox who steals from the rich to give to the poor. He is an expert archer, a master of disguise, and a constant thorn in the side of villainous Prince John. Many ordinary folk are inspired by his daring deeds, and some even join him as outlaws themselves.

Did you know?

Just like Merida in *Brave*, Robin Hood can land an arrow straight down the middle of another arrow!

Need to know

Likes: His merry band of outlaws
Dislikes: Prince John, taxes
LEGO debut (shown here): 71038 Disney 100 Series (2023)

BRUSHING UP
Robin has the same bushy tail shape as the Beast from a Beauty and the Beast set, but he wears it pointing up instead of down!

Prince John

Phony king of England

THIS CRAFTY CAT rules England while his brother, King Richard, is away. He is only interested in power and wealth and bullies everyone into giving him what little they have. Short-tempered and sulky, the prince is outraged when Robin Hood resists his reign and does all he can to get the outlaw locked up.

Need to know

Likes: Riches, sucking his thumb
Dislikes: Robin Hood, King Richard
LEGO debut (shown here): 71038 Disney 100 Series (2023)

Did you know?

The earliest known tales of Robin Hood were written in England more than 500 years ago!

Ariel

Coming in to land

THIS INQUISITIVE MERMAID princess is fascinated by life outside her undersea palace, especially in the above-water world. Ariel ignores her father's warning that she should never get involved with humans—then she falls in love with one! She makes a deal with a sea witch to become human, but just for three days.

Life on land

Ariel's human form features in Ariel's Celebration Boat (43191), where she wears a wedding dress and tiara.

Hidden treasure

Ariel's collectible Minifigure from 2016's Disney Series 1 (71012) comes with a jewel inside a clamshell piece.

Live-action look

This Ariel mini doll is based on the character's live-action look in the 2023 version of *The Little Mermaid*.

Animated again

The star of Ariel's Music Stage (43235) and Ariel's Crystal Cavern (43254) is based on the animated series *Ariel*.

Need to know

Likes: Exploring, singing
Dislikes: Rules, sharks
LEGO debut: 41052 Ariel's Magical Kiss (2014)
Mini doll shown: 43267 Princess Castle & Royal Pets (2025)

Prince Eric

Romantic royal

WHEN ARIEL FALLS in love with a human, she picks a good one! Prince Eric is kind, hard-working, and a hopeless romantic. He loves the sea and is a skilled sailor as well as a master musician, dancer, and horse rider. Eric loves Ariel from the moment they meet, but he doesn't realize she is a mermaid!

Did you know?

The prince is not given a name in the Danish fairy tale that inspired Disney's *The Little Mermaid*.

Need to know

Likes: Ariel, his dog Max
Dislikes: Stormy seas
LEGO debut: 41052 Ariel's Magical Kiss (2014)
Mini doll shown: 43191 Ariel's Celebration Boat (2021)

Ready to sail

Prince Eric usually favors practical sailing clothes over formal wear, as seen in Ariel's Magical Kiss (41052).

Book of the film

Eric's micro doll appears in *The Little Mermaid* Story Book (43213), based on the 2023 live-action film.

Ariel's Animal Friends

Spanning land and sea

ARIEL'S CLOSEST COMPANIONS are underwater animals—and the occasional lucky land creature, too! Flounder the fish is always at Ariel's side when she explores the ocean in search of human treasure. Sebastian the crab prides himself on looking out for Ariel's safety, and Max the dog is just Max the dog!

Did you know?

In sets based on the live-action *The Little Mermaid*, Flounder is white with black and yellow stripes.

Ariel's Crystal Cavern (set 43254)

Flounder

Ariel's best friend is just as intrigued by the human world as she is, though he has no interest in swapping his tail for a pair of legs!

Sebastian

Ariel's father, King Triton, trusts this wise old crab to keep Ariel out of trouble—and to compose the kingdom's most pincer-snapping music!

Sebastian and Max: Ariel's Royal Celebration Boat (set 41153)

Max

Ariel is a little nervous around Prince Eric's pet sheepdog at first, but Max is devoted to her from the moment she saves his master's life.

Ursula

Tentacled terror

THIS SCHEMING SEA witch wants to rule the oceans and uses Ariel to advance her plans. She knows that if she has the princess in her power, King Triton will have to do whatever she demands. Ursula's dark magic lets her disguise herself as a human or grow to giant sea-monster size!

Did you know?

In Ariel and the Magical Spell (41145), Ariel comes with both a tail and legs so Ursula can perform her magic!

For the fangs

As a collectible Minifigure in 2016's Disney Series 1 (71012), Ursula flashes her pointed teeth and wields King Triton's trident!

Which witch?

The most recent Ursula minifigure shows her as Ariel's aunt from the live-action version of *The Little Mermaid* from 2023.

Aunty hero

Ariel's Aunt Ursula isn't a villain at all in the Disney Junior series *Ariel*, on which this "mer-gician" mini doll is based.

Need to know

Likes: Plotting, trickery
Dislikes: King Triton
LEGO debut: 71012 Disney Series 1 (2016)
Mini doll shown: 41145 Ariel and the Magical Spell (2017)

King Triton

Rules the waves

TRITON RULES THE underwater kingdom of Atlantica and is father to seven daughters, including Ariel and Arista. He is loving but strict and forbids his children—and all his subjects—from visiting the surface world of humans. Few dare disobey the king, but Ariel has a rebellious streak he cannot help but admire!

King Triton and Arista:
Ariel's Underwater Palace (set 43207)

Did you know?

In 1989's *The Little Mermaid*, Ariel's sisters' names all begin and end with "a": Attina, Alana, Adella, Aquata, Arista, and Andrina.

ARIEL HAS SIX older sisters, of which Arista is one of the youngest. None have much interest in the human world, preferring to make the most of life in Atlantica. Arista loves Ariel and occasionally joins in with her adventures, but she is happiest living by her father's rules and playing in the royal orchestra.

Arista

A-lister sister

Indira

Brinedive defender

Indira and Karina: The Little Mermaid Royal Clamshell (set 43225)

IN A WORLD where King Triton's daughters live and watch over seven different seas, Indira is protector of the warm and shallow Brinedive Sea. She is a kind and generous ruler and is celebrated for saving her people from a giant sea snake. She is also a skilled diplomat and a persuasive speaker.

INDIRA AND ARIEL'S sister Karina rules over the cold, northerly waters of the Saithe Sea. She is the most reclusive of King Triton's daughters and puts all her energy into looking after her realm's endangered creatures. Seeing the damage humans have done to the oceans has made her especially wary of the surface world.

Did you know?

In 2023's live-action *The Little Mermaid*, Ariel's sisters all have names ending with "a": Mala, Indira, Caspia, Tamika, Karina, and Perla.

Karina

Safe in Saithe

Belle

Loves tales as old as time

BOOK-LOVING BELLE is smart, brave, and independent. She makes her mind up about people based on their actions, not their appearances, and would do anything for the ones she loves. All those qualities win the heart of the Beast, who holds her captive in his castle, and help him turn back into a prince again.

Need to know

Likes: Books, horses, her father
Dislikes: Wolves, arrogance, Gaston
LEGO debut: 41067 Belle's Enchanted Castle (2016)
Mini doll shown: 43215 Disney 100 The Enchanted Treehouse (2023)

Did you know?

Belle has the rare distinction of being a LEGO mini doll, minifigure, micro doll, and LEGO DUPLO figure.

Blue Belle

Two variants of Belle's mini doll, both from 2021, depict the simple blue-and-white outfit she wears in her home village before she meets the Beast.

Gold standard

Most Belle mini dolls wear a wide version of her gold dress with printed rose and gathered fabric details. This one, with a broad smile, is from 2021.

A new look

Belle became a minifigure in 2024. The following year, an updated variant starred with the first minifigure Beast in 43263 Beauty and the Beast Castle.

The Beast

Not what he appears

THE BEAST DIDN'T always look like this! As a young and careless prince, he angered an enchantress who put a curse on him. Now he must fall in love—and be loved in return—before he can become a more thoughtful version of his former self. Will Belle be the one to transform his life?

BEAST NO MORE
In all his mini doll appearances, the Beast comes with a second head for turning him back into the Prince.

Need to know

Likes: Belle, ballroom dancing
Dislikes: Being judged by his appearance
LEGO debut: 41067 Belle's Enchanted Castle (2016)
Mini doll shown: 43196 Belle and the Beast's Castle (2021)

Have by the tail
This minifigure version doesn't wrap himself in a cape—all the better to show off his bushy tail!

BEAUTY AND THE BEAST

Gaston

Horrible hunter

THIS CRUEL AND arrogant hunter will go to any lengths to get his way. He wants to marry Belle, but she sees nothing to love in his brutish, bullying behavior. He is enraged to learn that she prefers the Beast to him and vows to destroy the cursed prince out of jealousy and spite.

Did you know?

The 2,916-piece Beauty and the Beast Castle (43263) is the biggest LEGO Disney set based on just one film.

GASTON'S SUCK-UP SIDEKICK tells him just what he wants to hear, yet even LeFou doubts his boss can win Belle's heart! He often plays the fool to make Gaston look good, but he is smart enough to know that his fortunes depend on doing what he is told.

LeFou

Gaston's go-to guy

BEAUTY AND THE BEAST

Maurice

Always inventing

BELLE'S FATHER LOVES to invent things and is always hopeful that his latest creation will be the one that changes their lives for the better. He doesn't care that people make fun of him, and wants Belle to tread her own path, too. He loves his daughter dearly and can't believe anyone would find her unusual.

BELLE AND MAURICE'S horse lived a simple life until the day Maurice led him down a cursed woodland path! Philippe turned tail and fled, leaving Maurice behind, but later found the courage to go back with Belle. Together they dodged wolves to find the Beast's enchanted castle—and the beginnings of a whole new life.

Philippe

Belle's way through the woods

Enchanted Castle Staff

Be their guest

WHEN A THOUGHTLESS prince turned an enchantress away from his door, she didn't just turn him into the Beast—she transformed everything around him, too! His luxurious castle became a forbidding fortress, and its gardens turned into dark and dangerous woods. Even his loyal staff were cursed to live as household objects!

Cogsworth

The Beast's most trusted advisor keeps the castle ticking along, even when the other staff members wind him up!

Cogsworth, Fifi, Lumière, Mrs. Potts, and Chip: Beauty and the Beast Castle (set 43263)

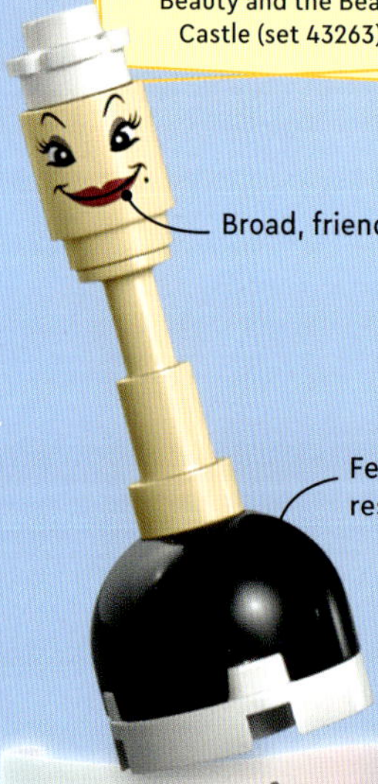

Fifi

It's hard work keeping an enchanted castle clean, but Fifi makes it look easy in her feather duster form!

Lumière

The castle's maître d' is a charismatic candelabra who helps light the flame of love between Belle and the Beast.

Mrs. Potts

Being turned into a teapot has done nothing to water down this wise housekeeper's kind and caring nature.

Chip

This inquisitive little teacup is Mrs. Potts's seven-year-old son and Belle's best friend among the castle staff.

Wardrobe

This kind-hearted cupboard sees the best in the Beast and comforts Belle when she fears that he might be a monster.

Wardrobe and Chef Bouche:
Belle and the Beast's Castle (set 43196)

Chef Bouche

The castle chef still loves preparing food, even as an oven! He runs a strict kitchen and hates to see food go to waste.

Aladdin

Wishing well?

QUICK-WITTED, FUN-LOVING Aladdin is happy with his life on the streets of Agrabah until he meets the runaway Princess Jasmine and falls in love. Convinced she could never love a street urchin, he uses a wish from a genie to become a prince. Jasmine is unimpressed, but the city's biggest villain, Jafar, is suitably enraged!

Need to know

Likes: Apples, Jasmine
Dislikes: Stealing, except to survive
LEGO debut (shown here):
41161 Aladdin and Jasmine's Palace Adventures (2019)

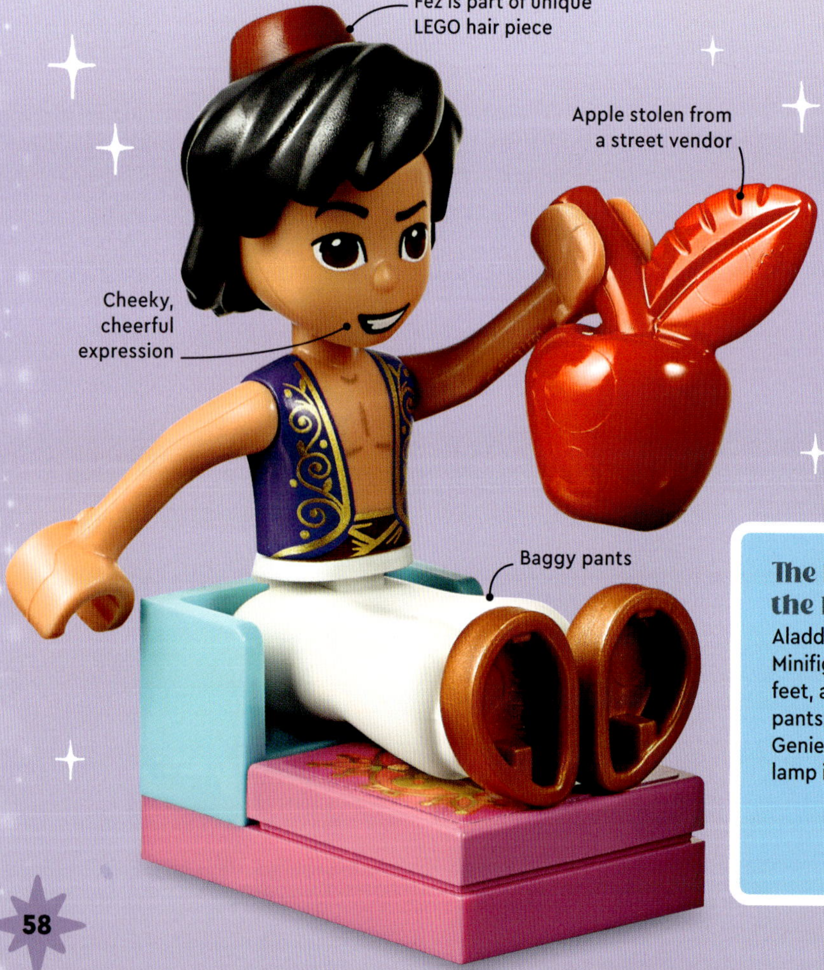

Did you know?

When Aladdin pretends to be a rich visiting royal, he calls himself "Prince Ali."

The lad with the lamp

Aladdin's collectible Minifigure has bare feet, a patch on his pants, and the Genie's magic lamp in his hand.

Jasmine

Princess of the people

THE PRINCESS OF AGRABAH lives a life full of luxury but lacking in excitement. She has no interest in the many princes lining up to meet her and would much rather be exploring the city's vibrant streets. Here, she meets Aladdin and steps into a wider world full of magic, adventure, love, and freedom.

Did you know?

In the Princess Enchanted Journey set (43216), Jasmine takes a baby elephant on a magic carpet ride!

Need to know

Likes: Animals, Aladdin
Dislikes: Being told what to do
LEGO debut: 41061 Jasmine's Exotic Palace (2015)
Mini doll shown here: 43216 Princess Enchanted Journey (2023)

Flyaway friend

In collectible Minifigure form, Jasmine has printed shoulder strap and shoe details plus a white dove for company.

The Genie

Your wish is his command

FEW BEINGS ARE as powerful as this wish-granting wisp of boundless blue energy! Set him free from his lamp and he will grant you three wishes—but when those wishes are spent, he must return to his lamp until summoned by someone else. He can live inside it for thousands of years at a time!

Did you know?

To date, the Genie's lamp has featured in 10 LEGO Disney sets, but the Genie is found in just one!

Need to know

Likes: Jokes, impressions, freedom
Dislikes: Being in his lamp for too long
LEGO debut (shown here): 71012 Disney Series 1 (2016)

WORK OF ART
In the LEGO Disney art set 100 Years of Disney Animation Icons (43221), the Genie is shown as a blue wisp coming from a lamp.

Jafar

Villainous vizier

THIS SCHEMING PALACE ADVISOR is the second most powerful man in Agrabah—but he wants to be the first! He plans to marry Princess Jasmine and replace her father, the Sultan, as ruler. Jafar already uses hypnosis to get his way, and if he can get his hands on a genie's lamp, he plans to make himself all-powerful!

Did you know?

A vizier is a ruler's most senior advisor, with great influence over how a kingdom is run.

Need to know

Likes: Dark magic, power
Dislikes: Aladdin, the Sultan
LEGO debut (shown here): 71024 Disney Series 2 (2019)

Mean genie

When Jafar wishes he is a genie, he becomes a red one with rippling muscles, bright yellow eyes, and his own lamp!

The Magic Carpet

Flying flooring

Aladdin and Jasmine's Palace Adventures (set 41161)

Mini dolls can ride on rare, curved LEGO rug piece

Intricate woven design with tigers in each corner

Gold tassels hang at each corner

ALADDIN MEETS THIS remarkable rug while looking for the Genie's lamp. The Carpet gladly helps him find it, then becomes his flying best friend. When Aladdin wants to impress Princess Jasmine, the Carpet treats them to an unforgettable nighttime flight, and it whisks them away again when the happy couple decide to marry.

Rajah

Putting the grrr in Agrabah

PRINCESS JASMINE HAS loved this Bengal tiger ever since she was a child and he was a cub. At times in her lonely palace life, he was her only friend, as well as her protector. Rajah is sad when Jasmine finally leaves the palace, but he still helps her on her way, knowing it is something she has to do.

Did you know?

Rajah appears as a tiger cub in 2025's LEGO Disney Princess Castle & Royal Pets set (43267).

Jasmine and Mulan's Adventure (set 43208)

Figure is almost as tall as a mini doll

Tail curls protectively around Jasmine

Big, princess-defending paws!

Simba

In the circle of life

Did you know?

Young Simba is made from 1,445 LEGO pieces and stands just over 11.5 in (29 cm) tall—almost as tall as a newborn lion cub!

ONE DAY, this cub will become the Lion King. As he grows, he will learn about loss, betrayal, and the all-important Circle of Life. But for now, he gets to play, make friends, and explore the African Pride Lands. His bright, innocent eyes see wonder everywhere—especially in the wisdom and majesty of his father, Mufasa.

KINGDOM TO COME

This minifigure-scale Simba gazes out from a brick-built Pride Rock in the LEGO Ideas set Magic of Disney (21352).

Need to know

Likes: Showing off, pouncing
Dislikes: Grooming, hyenas
LEGO debut (shown here): 43247 Young Simba the Lion King (2024)

Pocahontas

Peace-making princess

WHEN ENGLISH SETTLERS arrive in her homeland, Pocahontas is all that stands between war and peace. She forms a bond with Englishman John Smith, but this angers the other settlers and members of her own tribe. She puts herself in harm's way to speak out against hatred, and saves John's life in the process.

Did you know?

Pocahontas is one of 13 mini dolls in The Enchanted Treehouse—more than in any other LEGO set!

Need to know

Likes: Exploring, canoeing, nature
Dislikes: Closed-mindedness
LEGO debut: 71038 Disney 100 Series (2023)
Mini doll shown: 43215 Disney 100 The Enchanted Treehouse (2023)

Following her heart

The Pocahontas collectible Minifigure comes with John Smith's compass and three LEGO leaves, reflecting her love of nature.

Meeko

Ravenous raccoon

MISCHIEVOUS MEEKO IS one of Pocahontas's many animal friends. When he isn't eating, he is usually on the lookout for food and doesn't really care where it comes from. He helps Pocahontas learn to trust John Smith, but he takes his time to befriend the settlers' pug, Percy, preferring to steal his dog cookies!

POCAHONTAS MEETS this refined canine when he arrives on her shores with the English settlers. He belongs to the settlers' leader, Governor Ratcliffe, and is showered with care and attention by Ratcliffe's servant. Percy enjoys his luxury lifestyle, but he gives it all up to be with his new friends, Pocahontas and Meeko.

Did you know?

In Disney Duos (43226), Meeko and Percy share a display stand with a Disney 100 emblem.

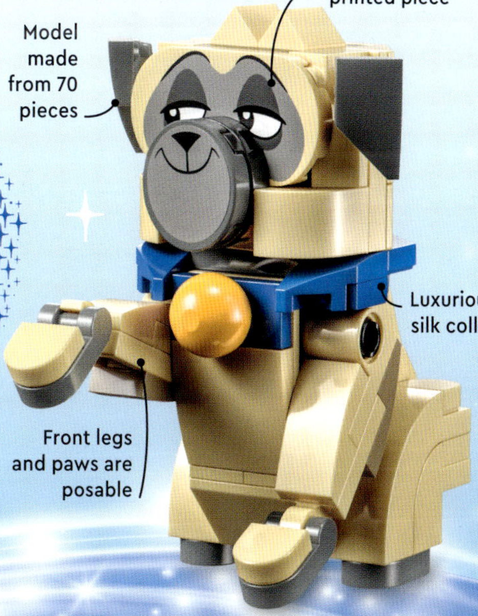

Percy

Pampered pug

Woody

Star sheriff

THIS CLASSIC COWBOY toy is no ordinary plaything. When his owner isn't looking, he leads his fellow toys on amazing adventures and cheers them up when they're feeling down. He was made a long time ago—when cowboy toys were all the rage—and has been passed down from one lucky child to the next.

Tall story

The first LEGO® Toy Story™ sets mixed minifigures with all-new figure types. This 2010 Woody has a custom head with a built-in hat and extra-long limbs.

Grime time

Woody has good reason for looking so glum and grubby here. He's just escaped from the trash compactor in a 2010 set based on *Toy Story 3*!

Need to know

Likes: Playing with his owner
Dislikes: Losing his hat
LEGO debut: 7590 Woody and Buzz to the Rescue (2010)
Minifigure shown: 43212 Disney Celebration Train (2023)

Buzz Lightyear

To infinity and beyond!

WOODY'S BEST FRIEND is the most modern toy in the toy box. His light and sound effects are so impressive that he even believed he was a real Space Ranger for a while! Now that he knows he is an action figure, he loves nothing more than life on Earth with a loving owner and some plaything pals.

Need to know

Likes: Flying, adventures
Dislikes: Being on demo mode
LEGO debut: 7590 Woody and Buzz to the Rescue (2010)
Minifigure shown: 43264 Toy Story Celebration Train & RC Car (2025)

Did you know?

Buzz forgets he's a toy when switched to demo mode—and becomes a great dancer in Spanish mode!

Under the dome

The first Buzz minifigure has a unique head shape and a rounder wingsuit with a domed helmet and shorter wings. He features in four 2010 sets.

Jessie

Collectible cowgirl

THIS YODELING COWGIRL is part of the same range of toys as Woody. She was ready to spend her life in a toy museum until Woody and Buzz reminded her what it feels like to have a child to play with. Now she's a much-loved part of Woody's gang, ready to lead the way on new adventures.

Need to know

Likes: Animals, yodeling
Dislikes: Being left behind
LEGO debut: 7594 Woody's Roundup! (2010)
Minifigure shown: 43264 Toy Story Celebration Train & RC Car (2025)

Did you know?

Jessie is proud to be a rare and sought-after toy based on a 1950s TV puppet show called *Woody's Roundup*.

Big Jessie

This tall Jessie figure features in two LEGO Toy Story sets from 2010, both of which also come with Woody and his trusty toy horse, Bullseye.

Rex

Trusty toy-rannosaur

THIS TYRANNOSAURUS REX toy has a tiny roar but a huge heart. He has a trusting nature and a talent for video games. What he lacks in confidence he makes up for in kindness—and occasional clumsiness. But hey, it's not easy having an enormous tail that sends everything flying whenever he spins around in surprise.

THERE'S MORE THAN just money inside this playful piggy bank. Hamm is packed full of facts, wisecracks, and well-earned confidence. When his fellow toys need to know about the outside world, they turn to this treasury of trivia. And even if they don't need to know, there's a good chance he'll chime in anyway!

Did you know?

Hamm is great at playing a villain and wears a black hat to become the evil Dr. Porkchop!

Hamm

Knowledge bank

Bo Peep

Looking out for her flock

NO TOY GETS left behind when this shepherd is on the case. By hook or by crook, she'll do what it takes to help lost playthings find a home. She started life as part of a lamp but soon found her place with Woody and his pals. Bo Peep may be made of porcelain, but she never cracks under pressure.

THESE TOY TROOPERS prove that even small toys can be a force to be reckoned with. Stationed inside a Bucket O' Soldiers, they are ready to serve their fellow toys—whether it's by standing up to bigger toys or heading out on a stealth mission to find out about life beyond their owner's bedroom.

Army Guys

The thin green line

Bullseye

Trusty steed

EVERY COWBOY NEEDS a horse, and Woody is proud to share this one with Jessie. Bullseye is devoted to the two of them and makes his feelings known by behaving like a playful puppy dog. When he needs to act like a horse, however, this steed can speed like a champion racer.

THIS REMOTE-CONTROL car loves nothing more than taking other toys for a high-speed ride. Give him a destination, fresh batteries, and a boost of turbo mode, and he'll get you where you need to go. At his best, he's as fast as a full-size car, and he's always got room for one more passenger.

RC

Driving force

Friendly Figures

Here to help Woody and Buzz

NO TRIP OUTSIDE the toy box is complete unless Woody and Buzz make a few new friends! The pair made contact with aliens at the Pizza Planet restaurant, and Woody met Forky at Bonnie's kindergarten. Buzz befriended Ducky and Bunny at a traveling carnival before he and Woody had a blast with Duke Caboom.

Aliens

Woody and Buzz have met hundreds of these otherworldly beings, and three have become their unshakable friends.

Forky

Bonnie made this toy all by herself! At first, he thinks he belongs in the trash, but Woody helps him see things differently.

Aliens and Forky: RV Vacation (set 10769)

Buzz & Woody's Carnival Mania! (set 10770)

Ducky and Bunny

These plush pals always stick together. They hung out as unclaimed carnival prizes until they teamed up with Buzz.

Duke Caboom's Stunt Show (set 10767)

Duke Caboom

Just like Woody, Duke is a classic toy from an earlier age. Unlike Woody, he'd rather ride a motorbike than a horse.

Zurg

Built to be bad

PART OF THE same toy range as Buzz Lightyear, Zurg is the sworn enemy of all Space Rangers. He believes he is an emperor from another world on a mission to control the galaxy. In fact, he is a battery-powered action figure whose greatest weapon is a harmless hand-held ball shooter!

THIS GRIZZLED GOLD prospector is bitter about being the least popular toy in the *Woody's Roundup* range. He has spent most of his life unloved and unsold and now thinks Woody, Jessie, and Bullseye should be made to spend their days stuck on a shelf with no children to play with, too!

Did you know?

Stinky Pete doesn't really stink—it's just his name from the *Woody's Roundup* TV show!

Stinky Pete

Roundup rogue

Lotso

Not-so-cuddly toy

WHEN HIS LOVING owner lost him, Lotso turned his strawberry-scented soul to evil. Now he rules the roost at Sunnyside Daycare center, making trouble for as many toys as possible. He is a big, bitter bully whose soft, wipe-clean fur hides a hard, ink-stained heart!

AFTER 60 YEARS gathering dust in an antique store, this downhearted doll is desperate to be loved. Her pull-string voice box has never worked properly, and she's sure it's the root of all her problems. She'll go to any lengths to get a new one, even if it means taking Woody's voice from him!

Did you know?

Lotso is the main villain in *Toy Story 3*, while Gabby Gabby features in *Toy Story 4*.

Gabby Gabby

Finding her voice

Lotso's Gang

Backing up the bear

WHEN BIG BAD Lotso tells the toys at Sunnyside Daycare what to do, he relies on his gang to make them do it! The boss bear has convinced his followers that children are their enemies, but deep down they would rather be playing with kids than propping up Lotso's rule.

Twitch

This mean, green action figure uses his giant insect eyes to spot anyone trying to escape from Sunnyside by night.

Stretch

The long arm of Lotso's law reaches into every corner, thanks to this octopus toy and her eight rubbery tentacles.

Chunk

Lotso's stony sidekick may be two-faced, but he doesn't hide it, rocking back and forth between two expressions.

Hercules

The man, the myth, the muscles

THIS ANCIENT GREEK warrior is a child of the gods, but he lost his place on Mount Olympus when he was a baby. To get it back, he must prove himself a true hero—not simply by seeing off monsters with his great physical strength, but by finding the inner strength of his heart.

Did you know?

The lightning bolt on Hercules' shield honors his father, Zeus, the god of thunder and lightning.

LABORED LOOKS
Hercules has a second, strained expression for when he takes on mighty tasks and faces down powerful foes.

Need to know

Likes: Epic quests
Dislikes: Hades
LEGO debut (shown here): 71024 Disney Series 2 (2019)

Hades

Uncle from the Underworld

Need to know

Likes: Scheming, schmoozing
Dislikes: Life in the Underworld
LEGO debut (shown here): 71024 Disney Series 2 (2019)

OF ALL THE GODS in Ancient Greece, Hercules' uncle is the most hot-headed. He is always plotting against his nephew and has a burning desire to be top god on Mount Olympus. It is his fault Hercules lost his place in the pantheon, and he would love to see him lose a lot more!

Did you know?

Hades is part of the same series of collectible Minifigures as his nephew, Hercules.

KEEP YOUR HAIR ON
Unlike most LEGO minifigures, Hades' head and hair are one piece, so no one can steal his flaming style!

Mulan

Disguised defender

FA MULAN LOVES her father so much that she takes his place when he is called up to fight an invasion. Living in a time when women aren't allowed to be soldiers in her country, she disguises herself as a young man and becomes the best recruit in her army unit. When the truth comes out, she is hailed as a hero.

Need to know

Likes: Animals, inventing, martial arts
Dislikes: Injustice, dishonor
LEGO debut: 41151 Mulan's Training Day (2018)
Mini doll shown: 43215 Disney 100 The Enchanted Treehouse (2023)

Did you know?

Fa Mulan is the first Disney Princess not to come from or join a royal family.

Daring disguise

Mulan, disguised as Ping, appears in one LEGO Disney Princess micro doll storybook set from 2020.

True blue

Mulan wears this outfit after she stops disguising herself and goes into battle as a woman for the first time.

Less Ping, more bling

Mulan's collectible Minifigure wears the medal-like crest awarded to her by the Emperor of China.

Mulan's Animal Friends

Creatures great and small

WHEN MULAN GOES to war, she takes her family's horse, Khan, with her but leaves her pet cricket, Cri-Kee, behind. Cri-Kee is not too pleased about that and convinces the family's former guardian spirit, Mushu the dragon, to go after her. Together, the three creatures help Mulan become a brave and celebrated soldier.

Khan

Mulan's horse is not convinced by her plan to become a soldier, but he still does all he can to make her mission a success.

Khan and Cri-Kee: Jasmine and Mulan's Adventure (set 43208)

Princess Castle and Royal Pets (set 43267)

Mushu

This diminutive dragon is desperate to prove himself in the eyes of Mulan's family and win back his place as their guardian spirit.

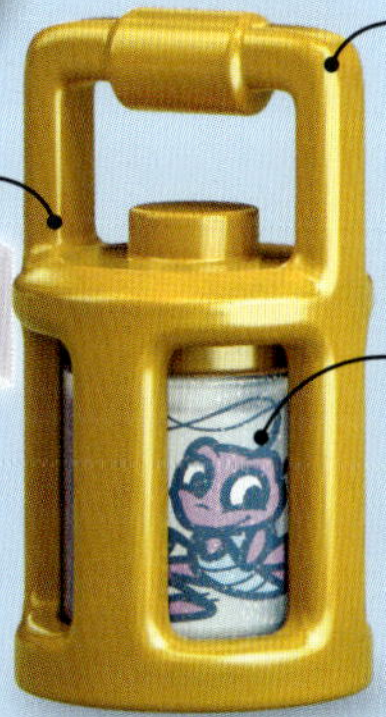

Cri-Kee

This "lucky" cricket is free to leave his cage but finds it a good place to go back to when his fortunes aren't so good!

Li Shang

Captain courageous

AS A TEENAGE CAPTAIN in the Imperial Chinese army, Li Shang is brave in battle and awkward in most other situations! When Mulan poses as a man, she wins his trust by saving his life, and when her true identity is revealed, he falls in love with her. They are eventually married by the dragon guardian Mushu.

Need to know

Likes: Mulan, martial arts
Dislikes: Breaking the rules
LEGO debut (shown here): 43174 Mulan's Storybook Adventures (2020)

Did you know?

Li is Shang's family name, just as Mulan's family name is Fa (which can also be spelled "Hua").

AN OPEN BOOK
Li Shang is one of three LEGO micro dolls in Mulan's Storybook Adventures (43174), a playset that opens and closes like a book.

Lilo

Stitch's best friend

LIFE ISN'T EASY for orphaned sisters Lilo and Nani Pelekai—and it gets even more complicated when Lilo adopts a dog that is really an alien! Stitch's antics turn six-year-old Lilo's world upside down, but for the first time ever, she has a best friend who doesn't think she's the weird and disruptive one!

Need to know

Likes: Family, photography, surfing
Dislikes: Baths, being captured
LEGO debut: 21352 Magic of Disney (2024)
Minifigure shown: 43268 Lilo and Stitch Beach House (2025)

SUN, SEA, AND SPACESHIPS
Lilo and Nani's Hawaii home is recreated in Lilo and Stitch Beach House (43268). The set also comes with a spaceship for Stitch!

Did you know?

Lilo's minifigure has the same LEGO hair piece as Mulan's mini doll. Mulan can also wear a flower.

Stitch

Experiment 626

THIS MINIATURE MONSTER was made in a lab by an alien scientist. He is genetically engineered to be super-strong, super-smart, and super-destructive! On Earth, he was mistaken for a stray dog and adopted by a young girl named Lilo. Now Lilo and Stitch are inseparable and living happily in Hawaii.

Need to know

Likes: Lilo, music, surfing
Dislikes: Baths, being captured
LEGO debut: 71012 Disney Series 1 (2016)
Minifigure shown: 43268 Lilo and Stitch Beach House (2025)

Heavily armed

Stitch has four arms, but he usually keeps two hidden. Here, he wears an alien spacesuit with sleeves for all four.

BIG TROUBLE
This scaled-up Stitch (43249) is made from 730 LEGO pieces. His head and ears are posable, and he can wear a flower in his fur.

Nani

Looking out for Lilo

Did you know?

Nani has a Mulan poster on her wall in the LEGO Disney Lilo and Stitch Beach House (set 43268).

LILO'S GROWN-UP SISTER has a busy life trying to hold down a job, look after Lilo, and prove to social worker Cobra Bubbles that their home is a fit place to raise a child. When Stitch joins the family, things get even more hectic, but Nani always finds time to do the right thing by her loved ones.

Nani and David: Lilo and Stitch Beach House (set 43268)

THIS PELEKAI FAMILY FRIEND is a daring fire dancer and skilled surfer. He is like a big brother to Lilo and would like to be Nani's boyfriend. He doesn't want to rush things, though, and is happy to wait for Nani's life to calm down ... which will surely happen one day, won't it?

David

Carrying a torch for Nani

Cobra Bubbles

Secret agent social worker

IF THIS SOCIAL WORKER looks more like a CIA agent, it's because that's exactly what he used to be! Having had enough of secret missions involving aliens, he moved into social services, only to meet another space invader named Stitch! He is strict but fair in his dealings with humans and aliens alike.

ANGEL IS PART of the same illegal experiment that created Stitch. But where he was designed to cause chaos, she was genetically engineered to turn people into villains with her singing voice! When she met Stitch, they fell in love and she changed her ways, performing her songs for entertainment, not evil.

Did you know?

Angel was first seen in *Lilo and Stitch: The Series* in 2004 and became a LEGO model in 2025.

Angel

Experiment 624

Nemo

Found fish

Did you know?

Nemo and Squirt are among the famous pairs in a 2023 set called Disney Duos (43226).

WHEN THIS YOUNG CLOWNFISH is caught by divers, his father embarks on an epic quest to find him. They are reunited in Sydney, Australia, where Nemo makes a daring escape from a dentist's aquarium! Later, he teams up with his dad on a mission to the US to track down their missing friend, Dory.

Nemo and Squirt: Disney Duos (set 43226)

THIS PLUCKY YOUNG sea turtle has no trouble coming out of his shell! He is one of many animals befriended by Nemo's dad, Marlin, on his mission to find his missing son, and he later becomes friends with Nemo, too. In fact, Squirt gets along with almost every ocean creature from coast to coast.

Squirt

Intrepid turtle

Mr. Incredible

Super-strong super dad

AS A YOUNG MAN, Mr. Incredible was one of the world's most famous super heroes. But when "supers" were banned, he settled down to become plain old Bob Parr, raising a family and working in an office. When he finally gets back into his super-suit, he brings his whole family along for the adventure.

Poster boy

Mr. Incredible's collectible Minifigure comes with a poster piece showing him as a young super hero in a blue uniform.

Did you know?

The Incredibles movies are set back to back, despite a 14-year gap between them in the real world.

Need to know

Likes: Peace, justice, cakes
Dislikes: The ban on super heroes
LEGO debut: 71012 Series 1 (2016)
Minifigure shown: 10760 Underminer Bank Heist (2018)

Elastigirl

Mrs. Incredible

EARTH'S STRETCHIEST SUPER HERO has her arms full raising three super kids with her husband, Mr. Incredible. Her far-reaching powers come in handy around the house, and she gives great hugs, but Helen Parr is truly at her best when stretched a little further. If trouble rears its head, she'll be ready to tangle with it!

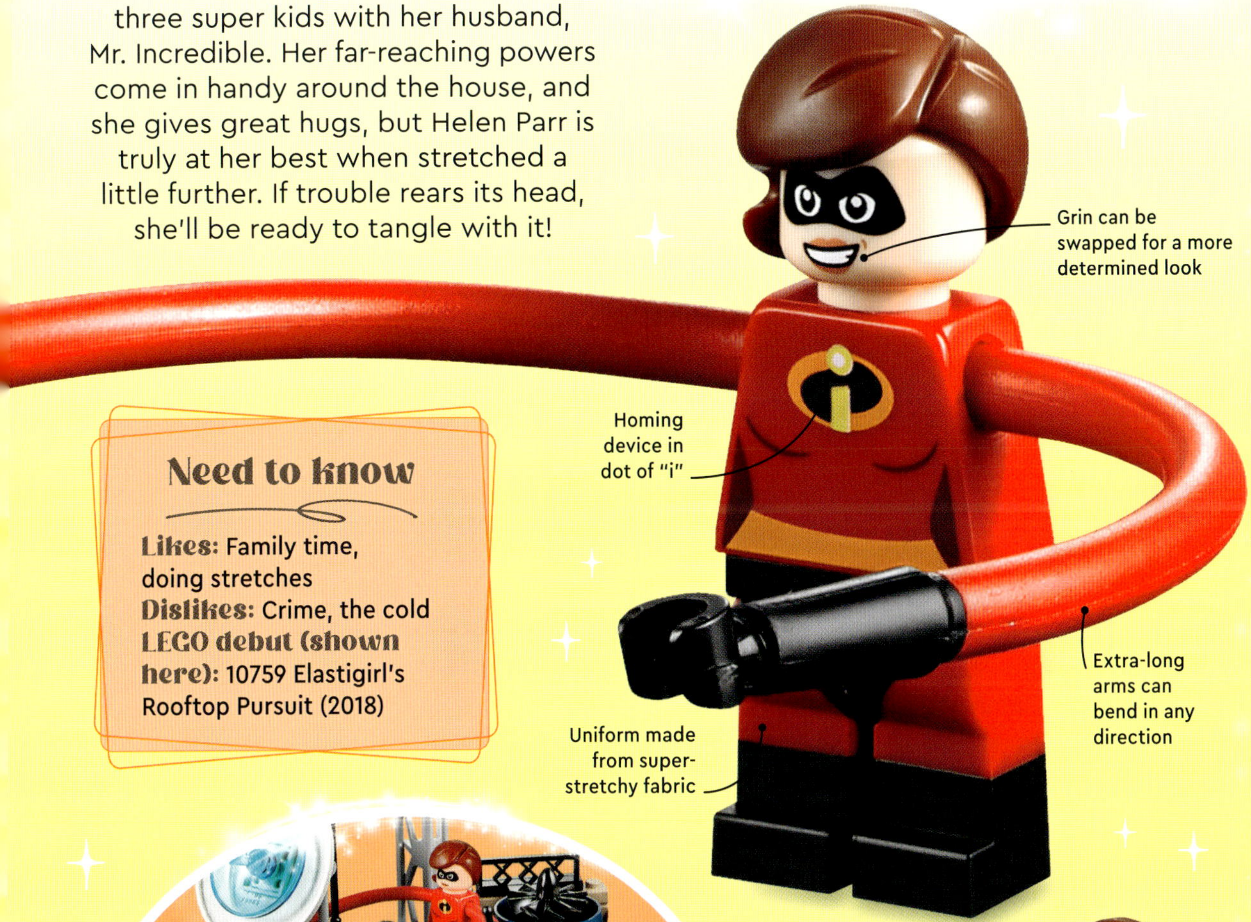

Need to know

Likes: Family time, doing stretches
Dislikes: Crime, the cold
LEGO debut (shown here): 10759 Elastigirl's Rooftop Pursuit (2018)

ARM'S LENGTH
The arms on this Elastigirl minifigure are made from one long LEGO piece. Pulling on either arm makes it longer as the other gets shorter.

Helping hands

An Elastigirl minifigure with standard arms teams up with Mr. Incredible in the LEGO® Juniors set Underminer Bank Heist (10760).

Violet Parr

Transparent teen

LIKE A LOT of teenagers, Mr. Incredible and Elastigirl's eldest child feels like she doesn't fit in. Vi would love to turn invisible and cocoon herself in a protective force field—and, unlike other teens, she can! Her parents always told her to hide her powers ... until the day the world really, really needed them.

HOME INVASION
The Incredibles' residence comes under attack in The Great Home Escape (10761). The set includes their living room, swimming pool, and more.

Need to know

Likes: Not being seen (when invisible)
Dislikes: Not being seen (when visible)
LEGO debut (shown here): 10761 The Great Home Escape (2018)

Dash Parr

Boy racer

THE OLDER SON in the Incredibles' household is a super-fast showoff, eager to reveal his powers against the wishes of his parents. When he finally gets the chance to be a super hero, he speeds into action—running up walls and over water, and generally moving faster than a bad guy's eye!

Need to know

Likes: Sports, snacks, pranks
Dislikes: School detention—so slow!
LEGO debut (shown here): 10761 The Great Home Escape (2018)

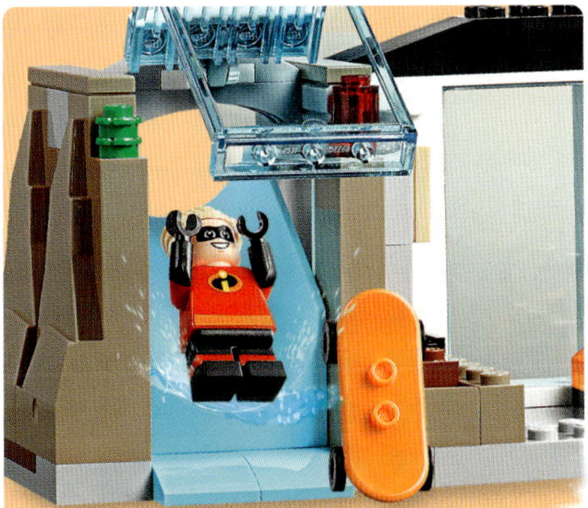

MAKING A SPLASH
Dash comes in a set featuring the Parrs's spectacular family home from *Incredibles 2*—complete with a waterfall to slide down.

Did you know?

So far, all the LEGO sets featuring the Parr family have been based on the film *Incredibles 2*.

Jack-Jack Parr

Incredible infant

LITTLE JACK-JACK is the newest member of the Incredibles clan, with more superpowers than the rest of the family put together. This turbo-charged toddler can make fire, move objects with his mind, pass through solid objects, teleport, and levitate. As if that isn't enough, he can also turn himself into metal, water, a giant, or a monster!

Edna Mode

Designer darling

THE FIRST-CHOICE fashion designer for super heroes is Edna Mode, an old friend of Mr. Incredible and Elastigirl. She makes custom and stylish suits using materials that can stretch, change size, stand up to explosions, and even turn invisible. She is always looking for new ways to innovate, but she draws the line at capes!

Frozone

Cold hands, warm heart

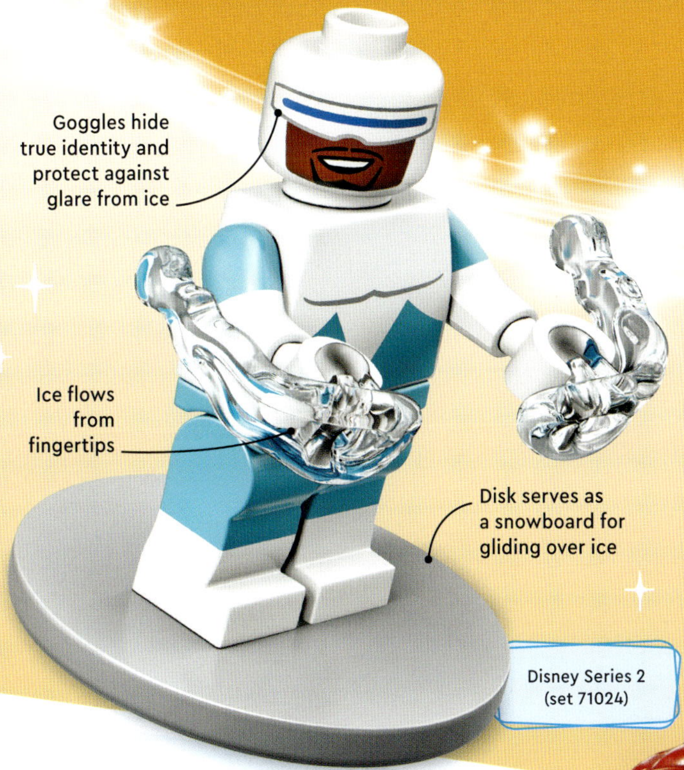

LUCIUS BEST IS a cool guy—so cool, he can make ice out of thin air, then slide along it! Before super heroes were outlawed, he teamed up with Mr. Incredible, and now he still loves to chill with him and his family. He doesn't get cold feet when they need him to don his Frozone costume once more.

AS HER SUPER HERO name suggests, Connie Mason stands as strong and firm as a brick wall! In her glory days, she was a barrier for bad guys, laying down the law and cutting off routes to crime. But she finds herself in conflict with the Incredibles when she is hypnotized by a new villain on the block.

Did you know?

Brick's biggest weakness is her fear of swimming—in water, she sinks like a stone!

Brick

Hard-headed hero

Syndrome

From fanboy to foe

AS A BOY, Buddy Pine dreamed of fighting crime as a super hero's sidekick. But when Mr. Incredible refused to let him put himself in danger, Buddy turned to villainy instead! Now he lives on an isolated island, making machines to fight super heroes and plotting his revenge against the Incredibles as Syndrome.

Need to know

Likes: Gadgets, power, revenge
Dislikes: Rejection, super heroes
LEGO debut (shown here): 71012 Disney Series 1 (2016)

Did you know?

Buddy's attempts to help Mr. Incredible are what got super heroes banned in the first place!

Flame-like hair suits fiery personality

Malevolent grin

Huge "S" for "Syndrome"

Plans for latest hero-fighting robot

Gloves packed with touch-control gadgets

Aero boots for rocket-powered flight

Underminer

Low-level threat

THIS MOLE-LIKE MENACE bursts out from underground to wreak havoc on the Incredibles' home town, Metroville. He is a self-declared enemy of peace and happiness and loves causing chaos just for the fun of it. He is also a fiendish bank thief, entering vaults from underneath and vacuuming up all the valuables.

Underminer Bank Heist (set 10670)

Elastigirl's Rooftop Pursuit (set 10759)

THE SCARY-LOOKING SCREENSLAVER is part of a plot to make super heroes look like villains. But when Elastigirl unmasks the seeming mastermind, she finds an ordinary delivery boy entranced by hypno-goggles. Whoever wears them becomes a puppet of the true Screenslaver, and Elastigirl knows they won't be stopped so easily.

Did you know?

The real Screenslaver can hypnotize victims using any screen, not just hypno-goggles.

Screenslaver

Boggled by goggles

Lightning McQueen

Faster than fast, quicker than quick

WINNING WAS THE only thing that mattered to this rookie racecar, until he came to the small town of Radiator Springs. Here, he learned what it meant to have friends and how to be a good friend in return. Now he's a champion on and off the track, picking up pals and prizes wherever he goes!

Need to know

Likes: Speed, travel, fair play
Dislikes: Cheats, clowns
LEGO debut: 5813 Lightning McQueen (2010)
Figure shown: 77255 LEGO® Speed Champions Lightning McQueen

Rust-eze bumper ointment sponsors Lightning's racing career

Lightning nearly always races as car 95

Model is made from 270 LEGO pieces, including four rubber tires

Did you know?

Lots of new LEGO parts were designed to recreate the characters from the *Cars* film series.

Unclean McQueen

Lightning cakes himself in mud and calls himself Chester Whipplefilter to compete in a demolition derby as car 15!

Bolt of blue

When Lightning becomes a racing crew chief, he gets an all-new paint job inspired by his old chief and mentor, Doc Hudson.

Mack

Keeps on trucking

LIGHTNING MCQUEEN'S OLDEST friend might also be his longest! With a trailer on his back, Mack hauls Team McQueen from track to track, giving the champion racer time to rest and recuperate. He may not be as fast as Lightning, but he rumbles like thunder as he stays safely within the legal speed limit!

Mack's Team Truck (set 8486)

Cruz Ramirez Race Simulator (set 10731)

THIS RAY OF SUNSHINE grew up watching Lightning McQueen race and decided to follow in his tire tracks. She is thrilled when she gets to train with him, and they soon bring out the best in one another. Cruz becomes the champion she always dreamed of being, and Lightning finds a new role as her trusted mentor.

Cruz Ramirez

Struck by Lightning

Cars of Radiator Springs

Lightning's home team

SLEEPY RADIATOR SPRINGS gets a rude awakening when Lightning McQueen ruins its main road on his way to a race! Over the next few days, as he works to fix the damage he caused, he falls in love with the Arizona town and its friendly residents. He makes it his home, and the locals become his biggest fans.

Sheriff

When Lightning first races into Radiator Springs, this police car is on hand to greet him—and to arrest him for tearing up the road!

Tow Mater

This rusty old tow truck runs a salvage yard in Radiator Springs. He is quick to see the good in Lightning and becomes his race crew chief.

Did you know?

Radiator Springs is located just off the historic Route 66, in Ornament Valley, Carburetor County.

Luigi and Guido

These best friends run a tire shop in Radiator Springs. They are big racing fans and jump at the chance to join Lightning's pit crew.

Sally Carrera, Flo, Fillmore, and Sarge: Flo's V8 Cafe (set 8487)

Sally Carrera

Lightning falls for this Radiator Springs attorney as soon as he meets her. It takes a while before she feels the same about him!

Flo

The oil and gasoline just keep on coming at Flo's V8 Café, Radiator Springs' most popular meeting place for more than 40 years!

Fillmore

The town's resident hippie believes in peace, love, and home-brewed biofuel. Somehow, he stays best friends with buttoned-up Sarge!

Sarge

This antique army jeep owns Sarge's Surplus Hut, Radiator Springs' one-stop shop for survival gear and old soldiers' stories!

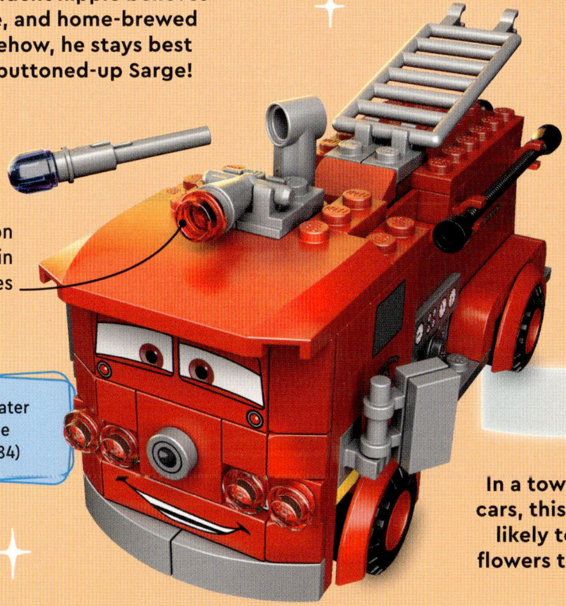

Red's Water Rescue (set 9484)

Red

In a town full of safety-conscious cars, this friendly fire truck is more likely to be found watering the flowers than fighting back a blaze!

World Grand Prix Cars

Best of the best

THE WORLD'S TOP RACECARS come together for the WGP (World Grand Prix). Lightning McQueen is proud to be among them, competing on tracks in Japan, Italy, and Great Britain. He has no idea the event is part of an evil plot, and neither do the other contestants. They just want to race and make their home countries proud!

Rear wing echoes flag design

World Grand Prix Racing Rivalry (set 8423)

Italian flag symbol on nose

Francesco Bernoulli

Lightning's main rival in the WGP is the most famous racecar in Italy. His livery says he is No. 1, and doesn't he know it!

Event branding on spoiler

Ultimate Race Set (set 9485)

GRC stands for Greatest Rally Car

Raoul ÇaRoule

This friendly French rally car is on a winning streak and likes his chances in the WGP—especially on the dirt road sections.

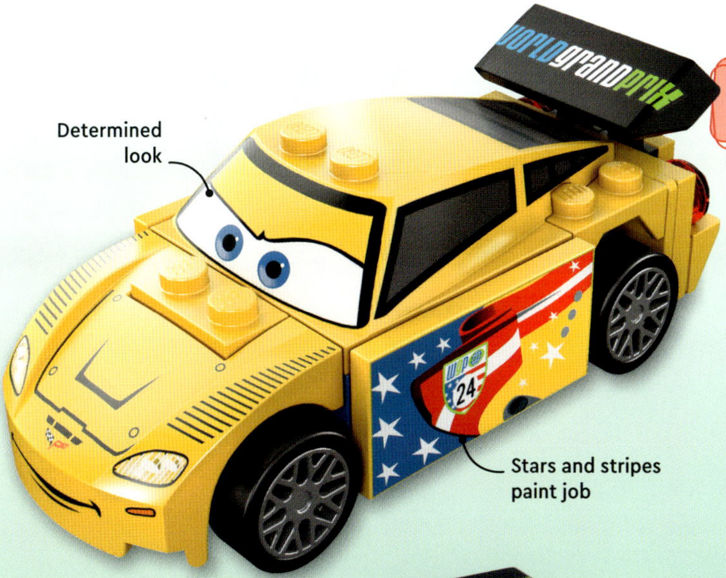

Jeff Gorvette (set 9481)

Jeff Gorvette

Lightning is good friends with this Californian car, but that doesn't mean they'll go easy on each other when they're on the track.

Ultimate Race Set (set 9485)

Max Schnell

Germany's greatest racer is as competitive as the next car, but has no time for conflict and likes to stay friends with all his rivals.

Tokyo International Circuit (set 8679)

Shu Todoroki

This compact Japanese racecar is inspired by his country's *Ka-riu* dragons—small but powerful creatures with a fiery nature!

Cars of England

On Her Majesty's secret service

LIGHTNING MCQUEEN and his friends from Radiator Springs come to London, England, for the final stage of the World Grand Prix. During their stay, they help the country's top spy cars uncover a conspiracy, expose the mastermind behind it, then take a trip to Buckingham Palace to meet Her Majesty the Queen!

Finn McMissile

This smooth-talking super-spy has gadgets for every occasion, from grappling hooks to pop-out hydrofoils.

Holley Shiftwell

Finn's sidekick is fresh out of spy school, but she has skills that even he is impressed by, such as the ability to fly.

The Queen

Britain's classiest car loves a day at the races and can't wait for the World Grand Prix to come to London.

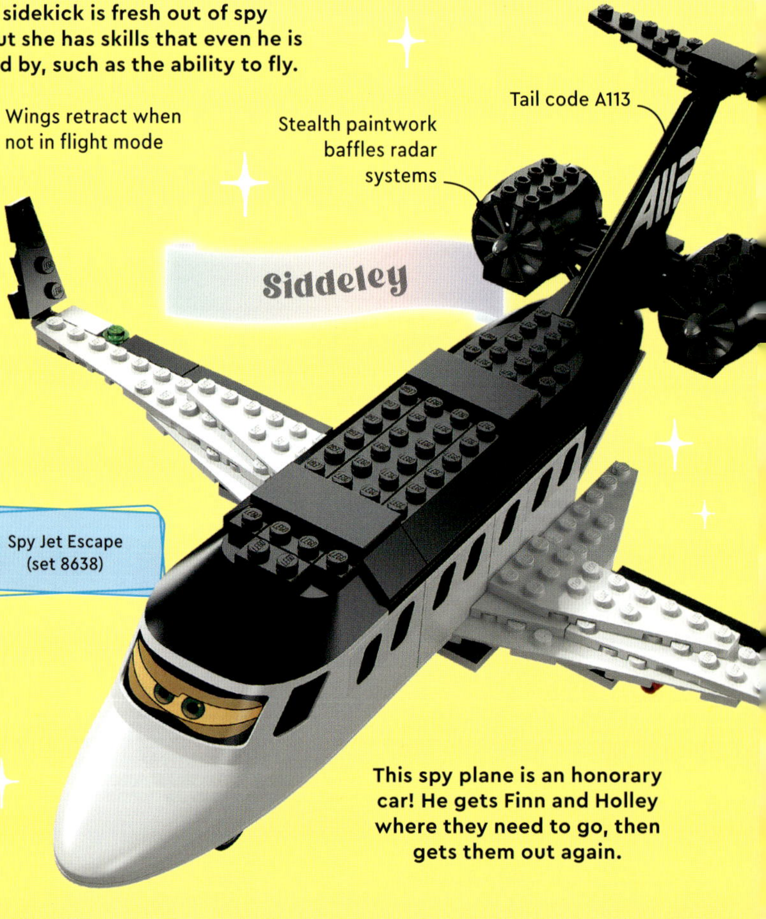

Siddeley

This spy plane is an honorary car! He gets Finn and Holley where they need to go, then gets them out again.

Lemons Conspiracy Cars

Out to wreck the WGP

Sir Miles Axlerod

This criminal mastermind claims he's invented an eco-friendly wonder fuel. But really it is highly explosive gasoline!

THESE VILLAINS AREN'T just out to disrupt the World Grand Prix—they're led by the car who set up the competition! Sir Miles Axlerod seems like a champion for environmentally friendly fuels, but really he wants to discredit them. If his clean-seeming contest turns into a disaster, he'll make a fortune from oil!

Professor Z

Axlerod's second-in-command makes the tech his boss needs to blow up racecars that run on his so-called superfuel.

Grem and Acer

These thugs take their orders from Professor Z. They love nothing more than being told to make some trouble.

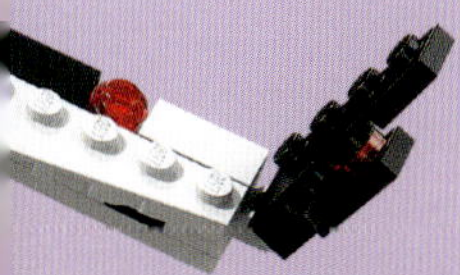

Petrov Trunkov

Like Grem and Acer, this bad guy hates his reputation as a "lemon"—a car with more faults than redeeming features!

Florida 500 Cars

Speedway stars old and new

THE BIGGEST PRIZE in speedway racing is the Piston Cup, and its most thrilling race is the Florida 500. To train for the event, Lightning McQueen must take courage from speedway heroes of the past, square up to the record-breaking car of the future, and learn a few lessons in a demolition derby!

Jackson Storm

Super-fast and super-arrogant, this next-gen racer has already set a speed record on the Florida 500 track!

Junior Moon

This classic car raced in the earliest days of the Piston Cup, and he now has a lifetime's worth of advice for Lightning.

Smokey

Lightning's latest crew chief is an ace mechanic who was prepping cars for the Piston Cup back in Junior Moon's day.

Miss Fritter

The rough and rowdy racing at this Florida 500 fan's demolition derby gives Lightning an unlikely kind of training!

WALL•E

Built to do humans' dirty work

AFTER 700 YEARS compacting trash with only a cockroach for company, this Waste Allocation Load Lifter—Earth-Class (WALL•E for short) is getting a little lonely. But then he meets EVE, a fellow robot on her own vital mission. She proves to WALL•E there is more to life on Earth than just endless mountains of trash!

Did you know?

The LEGO IDEAS WALL•E set (21303) was designed by the movie's lead animator, Angus MacLane!

TOGETHER AT LAST
In 2023, the LEGO BrickHeadz set EVE & WALL•E (40619) recreated Earth's greatest robot romance using just 155 pieces!

Need to know

Likes: EVE, the musical *Hello, Dolly!*
Dislikes: Loneliness, boredom
LEGO debut (shown here): 21303 WALL•E (2015)

EVE

To Earth with love

SENT TO EARTH in search of plant life, this Extraterrestrial Vegetation Evaluator shows little interest in WALL•E when they first meet. But when he saves her precious plant sample from being destroyed in space, something starts to grow between them. Sparks fly when they form a team, and their connection blossoms back on Earth!

EVE and M-O: WALL•E and EVE (set 43279)

Did you know?

The stars of *WALL•E* are united as a LEGO trio for the first time in the 2025 set WALL•E and EVE (43279).

THIS MICROBE OBLITERATOR'S to-do list is: clean, clean, clean! Unlike trash collector WALL•E, M-O's focus is on tiny specks of dirt and invisible germs—and if he senses either, he goes into a spin. When he meets WALL•E on the ultraclean starship *Axiom*, he is appalled by the older bot's centuries of accumulated filth!

M-O

Dirt detector

Tiana

Princess and a frog

THE BOSS OF Tiana's Palace restaurant didn't open her business overnight. It took years of hard work—and a brief period as a frog! She shared this fate with Prince Naveen, and the pair were only turned back into human beings when they fell in love, married, and shared a kiss in froggy form.

Did you know?

Before she became a princess, Tiana planned to call her restaurant "Tiana's Place."

Need to know

Likes: Cooking, live music
Dislikes: Shadow magic
LEGO debut: 41162 Ariel, Aurora, and Tiana's Royal Celebration (2019)
Mini doll shown: 43246 Market Adventure (2024)

Long hair worn up in a bun

Tiana loves music, especially jazz!

Magical gown made from leaves and lily pads

Dress skirt can be swapped for mini doll legs

Diamond dress

In 2022's set 43203, Tiana's "diamond" dress can also be used as a sparkling jewel-shaped mini doll carry case.

Crowned collectible

The collectible Minifigure Tiana (71038) has long gloves, a tiara, a Tiana's Place poster, and a LEGO frog accessory!

Prince Naveen

Twice transformed

THIS PARTY-LOVING PRINCE will do anything to avoid work and responsibility—even if that includes making a deal that sees him turned into a frog! In his four-legged form, he meets Tiana, who teaches him about the importance of doing things for other people. When he becomes a human again, he is a much improved one!

LEAPING HEARTS
The 2016 LEGO Disney Castle (71040) includes Naveen and Tiana in their frog forms, ready to share a life-changing kiss!

Need to know

Likes: Jazz, dancing
Dislikes: Being turned into a frog
LEGO debut (shown here): 43222 Disney Castle (2023)

PICTURE PERFECT
Naveen features in 2023's LEGO Disney Castle set, where he and Tiana can dance beneath a picture of the night they met.

Dr. Facilier

Dangerous to deal with

THIS CREEPY CON ARTIST promises to make all your dreams come true, but then he twists your wishes to his own devious ends! He makes his living in the back streets of New Orleans, but has big plans to rule the entire city. He tricks Prince Naveen into a terrible deal and tries to do the same with Tiana!

Need to know

Likes: Power, playing tricks
Dislikes: Being in anyone's debt
LEGO debut (shown here): 71038 Disney 100 Series (2023)

Did you know?

Facilier wears the same style LEGO hat as Jiminy Cricket, but in a different color and with printed details.

Hands on deck

Facilier's fateful deck of cards is represented by a unique LEGO tile depicting mystical minifigure hands with eyes!

Carl Fredricksen

At home and away

ALL HIS LIFE, Carl dreamed of being an explorer and seeing Paradise Falls in South America. It looked like it would never happen, until the day he tied 10,000 balloons to the roof of his house and flew it all the way there! Now he has a new outlook on life—after realizing he has been on a great adventure all along.

Need to know

Likes: Picnics, fireworks
Dislikes: Construction work
LEGO debut (shown here): 43217 "Up" House (2023)

CARL'S COMFORTS
The LEGO version of Carl's house has four detail-packed rooms that include pictures of his wife Ellie and their Paradise Falls savings jar.

Did you know?

Chip 'n Dale were the only animated Disney characters to have mid-length LEGO legs before Carl.

Russell

Accidental adventurer

Russell and Dug: "Up" House (set 43217)

THIS JUNIOR WILDERNESS Explorer has earned every merit badge there is, apart from the Assisting the Elderly one. To get it, he goes to help grumpy Carl Fredricksen at his home—just as the entire building flies away! Russell doesn't mean to hitch a ride, and Carl doesn't want him there, but they soon become best buds.

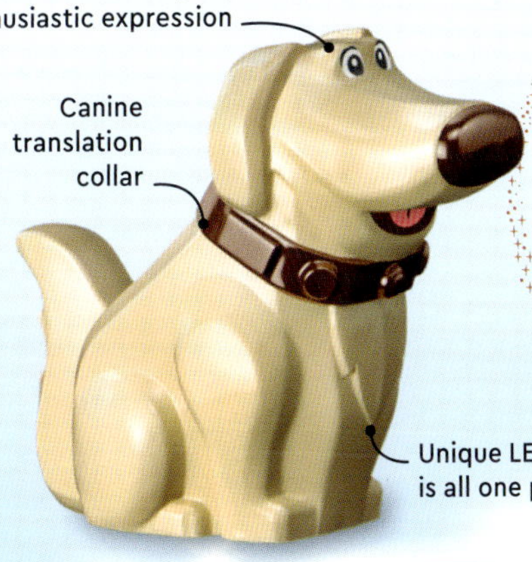

Did you know?

The LEGO Disney 100 "Up" House (43217) comes with a squirrel figure for Dug to chase!

DUG IS NO ORDINARY dog—he wears a collar that translates his thoughts into human speech! His master, the explorer Charles Muntz, has trained him to track down a very rare bird, but Dug is more interested in making friends. He meets Carl and Russell in Paradise Falls and becomes doggedly devoted to them both.

Dug

Speaks his mind

Rapunzel

Letting her hair down

AFTER STAYING INSIDE a tall, isolated tower for 18 years, Rapunzel is ready for some adventure. She goes in search of the sky lanterns that are released every year on her birthday and finds an entire kingdom full of new friends and excitement. She also finds out she is the kingdom's long-lost princess!

Did you know?

Multiple LEGO sets have featured Rapunzel's tower. The tallest is over 17 in (44 cm) high!

Need to know

Likes: Painting, proving herself
Dislikes: Captivity, shoes
LEGO debut: 41054 Rapunzel's Creativity Tower (2014)
Mini doll shown: 43241 Rapunzel's Tower & The Snuggly Duckling (2024)

Dressed to quest

Rapunzel wears this outfit to go on a quest beyond the kingdom in *Tangled: The Series*. It is found in just one LEGO set.

Brush with destiny

In minifigure form, Rapunzel comes with an artist's brush and palette for painting her beloved birthday lanterns.

Pascal

Warm-hearted lizard

THIS CHAMELEON IS Rapunzel's oldest friend, and for many years was her only true companion. He may be small, but he made her big, lonely tower feel a little less empty with his playful presence. He can also change color to blend in with his surroundings, which makes for good games of hide-and-seek!

Rapunzel's Tower & The Snuggly Duckling (set 43241)

RAPUNZEL'S HOME KINGDOM is protected by guards on highly trained horses—and Maximus is the most highly trained of them all. Before he met Rapunzel, he spent all his time galloping after villains. But now he admits to a softer side, and he can always be charmed with an apple!

Belle and Rapunzel's Royal Stables (set 43195)

Did you know?

When Rapunzel returns to her royal family, Maximus is made an officer in the palace guard.

Maximus

Galloping guard

Flynn Rider

Also known as Eugene

ONLY RAPUNZEL KNOWS the true story of this confident crook. Born Eugene Fitzherbert, he grew up reading tales of adventure starring fictional Flynnigan Rider. As a grown-up, he renamed himself Flynn Rider and lived only for thrills and personal gain. But a chance encounter in Rapunzel's tower turned his life around for the better.

MOST WANTED
Flynn doesn't feature in 2016's Rapunzel's Best Day Ever (41065), but his wanted poster does, complete with unflattering portrait!

Swag and swagger

Flynn's minifigure is well equipped for mischief, with his thief's swag bag and a choice of charming expressions!

Need to know

Likes: Rapunzel, his bad-boy reputation
Dislikes: Not looking his best on wanted posters
LEGO debut: 41054 Rapunzel's Creativity Tower (2014)
Mini doll shown: 43241 Rapunzel's Tower & The Snuggly Duckling (2024)

Mother Gothel

Not growing old gracefully

RAPUNZEL WAS RAISED by this selfish schemer, who pretended to be her mom. She shut the child away in a tower and tried to make her fear the outside world. As the years passed, Rapunzel grew older and wiser, but Gothel never changed. She jealously guarded Rapunzel and her enchanted hair to stay forever young.

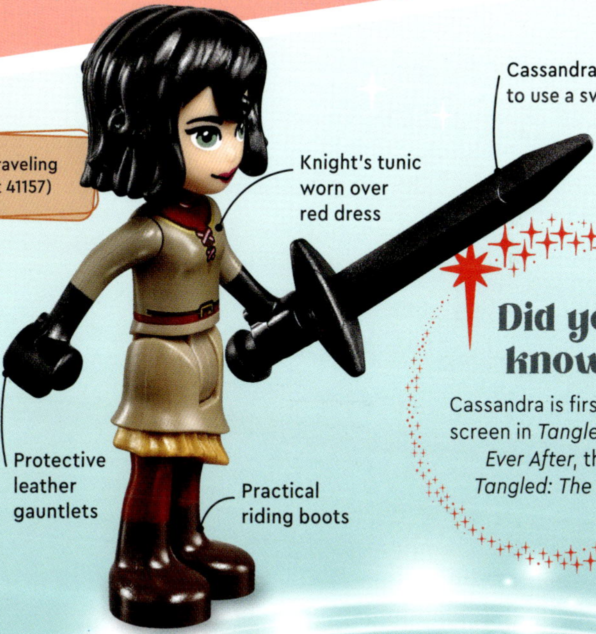

WHEN MOTHER GOTHEL took baby Rapunzel away from her family, she turned her back on her real daughter, Cassandra. She was found abandoned by the captain of the palace guard, who raised her to be smart, sassy, and skilled in combat. When she meets Rapunzel, they become firm friends and allies on countless adventures.

Did you know?

Cassandra is first seen on screen in *Tangled: Before Ever After*, then in *Tangled: The Series*.

Cassandra

Rapunzel's sort-of sister

Merida

Many strings to her bow

THERE'S NO BETTER archer in the Scottish Highlands than this sharp-shooting princess. She is rarely without her bow and arrow—even at the dinner table! Merida is also skilled with a sword, swift on horseback, and eager for adventure. She has no desire to be cooped up in a castle, trying to act refined and regal.

Did you know?

Merida is a princess of clan DunBroch, which is allied with clans Dingwall, MacGuffin, and Macintosh.

Brave new look

In 2022's Aurora, Merida and Tiana's Enchanted Creations (43203), Merida carries a standard bow, but is made from all-unique parts!

Need to know

Likes: Archery, her little brothers
Dislikes: Etiquette, tradition
LEGO debut (shown here): 41051 Merida's Highland Games (2014)

Harris, Hubert, and Hamish

Merida's bear-faced brothers

MERIDA'S THREE YOUNGER brothers never speak, but they always make their presence known around the castle. When not playing elaborate pranks, they can usually be found in the kitchen, looking for sweet treats to eat. Snacking on an enchanted cake turns them into baby bears, but it has no obvious effect on their behavior!

SNACK ATTACK
In Merida's Highland Games (41051), the princess can practice her archery skills while her brothers make mischief with a cookie launcher!

BEAR WITH ME
Merida's mom, Queen Elinor, also appears in bear form in a picture seen in Aurora, Merida and Tiana's Enchanted Creations (43203).

Elsa

Freed by fire in her heart

BORN WITH THE POWER to make ice and snow, Princess Elsa has spent most of her life hidden away for fear of harming others with her magic. When her love for her sister Anna finally lets her control her power, her life takes a new, more joyful path, and she embraces her future as the elemental Snow Queen.

Ready to rule?

There are two Elsa mini dolls in 2021's The Ice Castle (43197), including this one in her coronation gown and gloves.

Green queen

Elsa wears this green, flowery dress in Arendelle Castle Celebration (41068), inspired by the short film *Frozen Fever*.

Mighty white

As the mighty Snow Queen in one *Frozen II* set, Elsa lets her hair down and wears a white-and-lavender dress.

Cool collectible

In the second Disney series of collectible Minifigures (71024), Elsa wears her braided hair over her left shoulder.

Need to know

Likes: Anna, the Enchanted Forest
Dislikes: Isolation, hiding her feelings
LEGO debut: 41062 Elsa's Sparkling Ice Castle (2015)
Mini doll shown: 43244 Elsa's Ice Palace (2024)

Anna

Freed from ice in her heart

Did you know?

The *Frozen* film series is inspired by a 19th-century fairy story called *The Snow Queen.*

PRINCESS ANNA GREW UP with no idea why her beloved sister, Elsa, shut herself away from the world. On learning the truth, she risks everything to save Elsa from a life of cold isolation, and rescues the entire realm of Arendelle in the process! With her mission accomplished, she becomes her kingdom's queen.

Need to know

Likes: Elsa, Kristoff, magic
Dislikes: Loneliness, deceit
LEGO debut: 41062 Elsa's Sparkling Ice Castle (2015)
Mini doll shown: 43244 Elsa's Ice Palace (2024)

Sequel style

Anna wears her *Frozen II* traveling outfit in the Disney 100 celebration set The Enchanted Treehouse (43215) from 2023.

Summer greens

Anna's green summertime look is seen at the very end of *Frozen*, and variations on it appear in three LEGO Disney sets.

Braids on parade

Just like Elsa's collectible Minifigure, Anna wears her braids to the front in 2019's Disney Series 2 collection (71024).

Kristoff

Man of the mountains

RAISED BY ROCK TROLLS far from the royal palace, this hard-working mountain dweller has long relied on his reindeer for company. When he meets Princess Anna, he is inspired by how determined she is to save her sister, and falls in love with her. After he helps save Anna's life, the pair are engaged to be married.

Did you know?

The hidden mountain home of Kristoff's friendly troll family is called the Valley of the Living Rock.

Need to know

Likes: Anna, Sven, trolls
Dislikes: Wolves, unseasonal weather
LEGO debut: 41066 Anna & Kristoff's Sleigh Adventure (2016)
Mini doll shown: 43256 Anna's Sleigh Adventure (2025)

Special delivery

In 2019's Arendelle Castle Village set (41167), Kristoff wears his official ice master and deliverer uniform as seen in *Frozen II*.

Small change

In micro doll form, Kristoff dons his harvest festival costume from *Frozen II* and comes with a storybook-shaped carry case.

Sven

Sleighing it

RELIABLE REINDEER SVEN cannot talk, but Kristoff likes to pretend he can, putting on a voice that helps him work out how he feels about things. Sven, meanwhile, makes his true feelings clear with meaningful looks and emphatic snorts. He is Kristoff's constant companion and loyal co-worker in the ice delivery business.

Need to know

Likes: Kristoff, Olaf, carrots
Dislikes: Kristoff's comedy voices
LEGO debut: 41066 Anna & Kristoff's Sleigh Adventure (2016)
Figure shown: 43256 Anna's Sleigh Adventure (2025)

NEXT STOP: CHOCOLATE!
A carrot-chomping Sven takes Kristoff and Anna on a trip to a hot chocolate stand in Anna's Sleigh Adventure (43256).

A little deer
A smaller Sven appears in five sets, including the *Frozen*-themed LEGO Disney Advent Calendar 2025 (43273).

Olaf

Sun-loving snowman

Did you know?

Before he got his permafrost coating, Olaf relied on a personal snow cloud to keep him from melting away!

BORN OUT OF Elsa's magic, Olaf is an eternally optimistic snowman who finds wonder in everything and sees the best in everyone. Warm hugs, roaring fires, and sunny days at the beach especially melt his heart, but a magical permafrost coating makes sure he is never reduced to a puddle!

Need to know

Likes: Sunbathing, saunas
Dislikes: Having his head on upside down
LEGO debut: 41062 Elsa's Sparkling Ice Castle (2015)
Figure shown: 43265 Arendelle Frozen Castle (2025)

Build your snowman

In his early LEGO appearances, Olaf is a brick-built figure with twig pieces for arms and a dome-shaped brick base.

Heads together

In *Frozen* micro doll sets, Olaf's body is made from a unique version of the LEGO piece used to make minifigure heads.

Marshmallow

Elsa's enforcer

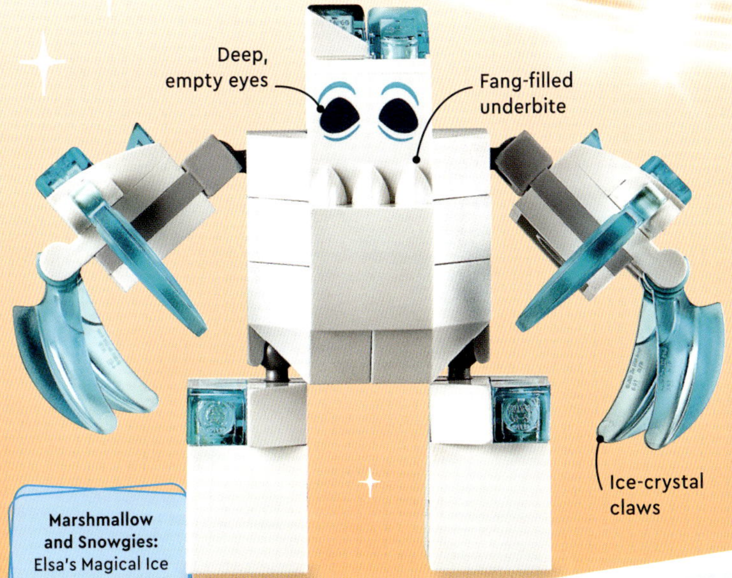

Marshmallow and Snowgies: Elsa's Magical Ice Palace (set 41148)

WHEN ELSA TOOK REFUGE in an isolated ice palace, she created this huge snow beast to keep everyone else away. The obedient giant gave Anna and Kristoff the cold shoulder before taking on a scarier, spiky form to fight off other visitors. He has since chilled out and now lives as king of the ice castle.

EVEN ELSA'S ILLNESSES are magical, and when she catches her first cold, every sneeze brings forth more of these miniature snow folk! The happy horde make mischief throughout Arendelle's royal palace before helping Anna celebrate her birthday, then moving in with Marshmallow at his mountain castle home.

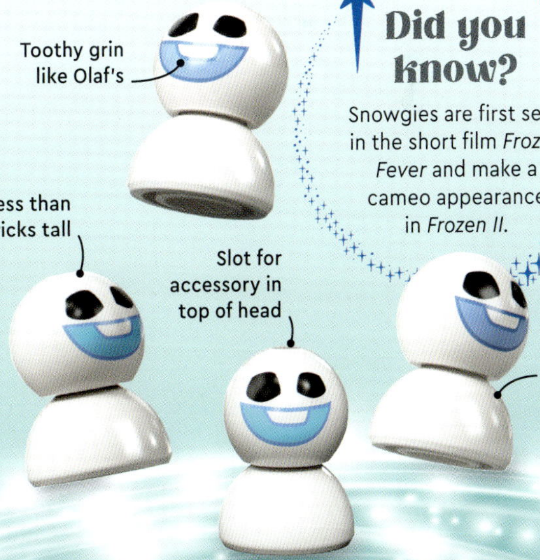

Did you know?

Snowgies are first seen in the short film *Frozen Fever* and make a cameo appearance in *Frozen II*.

Snowgies

Pleased to be sneezed

Lieutenant Mattias

Stranded soldier

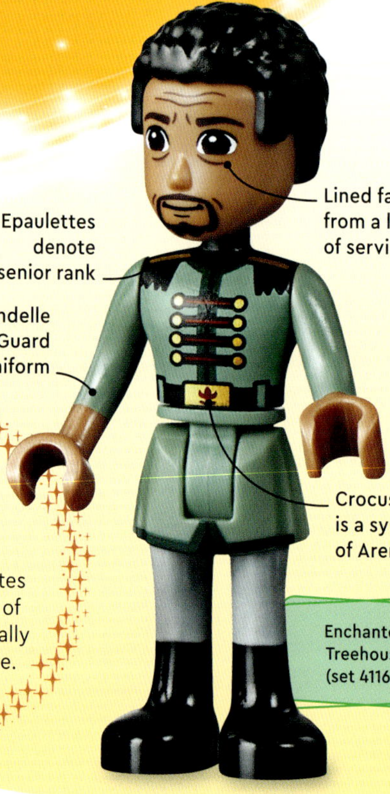

THIS LOYAL SOLDIER of Arendelle has not seen his home for 34 years. Tricked into fighting the friendly Northuldra people, Mattias and his troops angered the spirits of the Enchanted Forest and found themselves trapped within it. Elsa and Anna's arrival in the forest makes Mattias see the Northuldra and his orders in a different light.

Did you know?

Queen Anna promotes Mattias to the rank of general when he finally returns to Arendelle.

AS A YOUNG NORTHULDRAN, Honeymaren has never left the Enchanted Forest. She is distrustful of Mattias and the men who brought war to her home, which caused the elemental spirits to shut it off from the rest of the world. She longs to see the forest opened up again and to explore beyond its borders.

Honeymaren

Noble Northuldran

Queen Iduna

Missing mom

Did you know?

Queen Iduna and the brick-built Earth Giant are found in just one micro doll storybook set.

Queen Iduna and Earth Giant: Elsa and the Nokk Storybook Adventures (set 43189)

ANNA AND ELSA'S MOTHER grew up in the Enchanted Forest as a friend of the elemental spirits. She saved Prince Agnarr's life years before they became Arendelle's king and queen, and the spirits gave their first child magical powers as a reward for Iduna's bravery. Both Agnarr and Iduna were lost at sea many moons ago.

Earth Giants

Rock solid

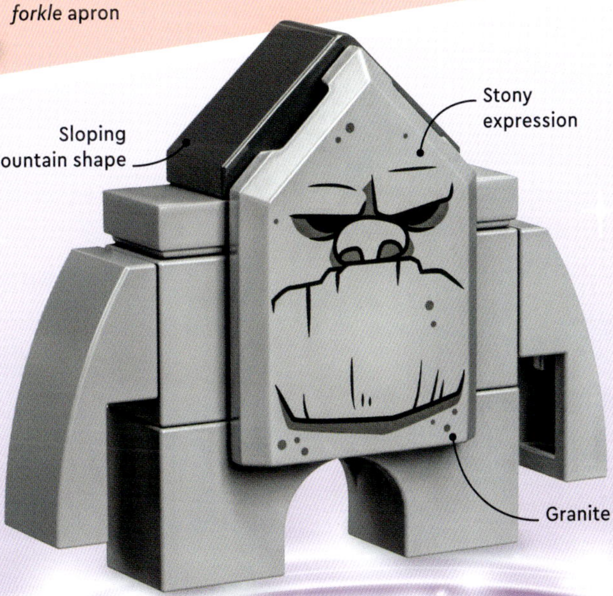

BY FAR THE BIGGEST of the elemental spirits in the Enchanted Forest, the Earth Giants are living mountains that move at night. Peaceful by nature, they turned against humankind when a former king of Arendelle harmed their home by building a giant dam. Even Elsa's magical powers cannot tame these enormous beasts!

Bruni

Spirited salamander

THE FIRE SPIRIT of the Enchanted Forest takes the form of a tiny salamander. In times of trouble, he fires off purple flames that quickly burn out of control. But when nature is in balance, his power can be harnessed for good. Together, Bruni and Elsa make a perfect team of fire and ice.

Elsa's Ice Castle & Snow Ride Adventure (set 43281)

THE ELEMENTAL SPIRIT of water takes the form of a majestic horse and guards the Dark Sea that lies within the Enchanted Forest. Elsa tames and befriends the Water Nokk, and it becomes her trusty steed. By sharing her ice powers with the liquid creature, it can become solid and travel on dry land.

Did you know?

Elsa rides a smaller Water Nokk with the same sparkly, opalescent effect in two micro doll sets.

Elsa and the Nokk's Ice Stable (set 43289)

The Water Nokk

Elemental equine

Baymax

Your personal health care companion

AT THE FIRST SOUND of distress, this inflatable medical robot explodes out of his travel case, ready to help! His calm, caring nature is programmed into a small control chip, along with the knowledge to treat almost any ailment. A few unconventional upgrades have also given him super-strength, a rocket fist, and the ability to fly!

Did you know?

Baymax returns to his travel case when he hears the words: "I am satisfied with my care."

Need to know

Likes: Helping, hugs
Dislikes: Health hazards
LEGO debut (shown here): 71038 Disney 100 Series (2023)

OUT OF THE BOX
When his help is needed, Baymax expands from a small red travel case, included with his collectible Minifigure.

Joy

Life of Riley

THIS FORCE OF POSITIVITY is one of many Emotions living in the mind of young Riley Andersen. As the first Emotion Riley ever experienced, Joy sometimes struggles to share Headquarters with the likes of Sadness, Anger, Fear, and Disgust. But if she occasionally pulls rank on the other Emotions, it's only to keep Riley happy!

Did you know?

There are thousands of yellow LEGO minifigures, but Joy is the first yellow mini doll!

Need to know

Likes: Riley, Goofball Island
Dislikes: Changes to Headquarters
LEGO debut (shown here): 43248 Inside Out 2 Mood Cubes (2024)

SHOW OF EMOTIONS
Joy's fellow Emotions are all represented in brick-built picture form in the Inside Out 2 Mood Cubes set (43248).

Anxiety

Fear of the future

Anxiety and Mind Workers: Inside Out 2 Mood Cubes (set 43248)

WHEN RILEY ANDERSEN turns 13, her head fills with strange new Emotions. The loudest voice belongs to Anxiety, a jittery bundle of overthinking energy that even Joy can't control. She is always planning for the worst, however unlikely, and won't let anyone else in Headquarters stop her. It's exhausting for Riley, and for Anxiety herself!

IT TAKES MORE than just Emotions to make up a mind! Hundreds of other workers staff Riley's synapses, taking care of dreaming, forgetting, imagining, and more. When she develops new Emotions, Riley's Mind Workers go into overdrive, expanding and upgrading the already impressive facilities in Headquarters.

Mind Workers

Emotional support

Moana

Master wayfinder

RAISED TO BE the next leader of her island and to never leave its shores, Moana breaks with tradition to follow the call of the ocean. She knows there can be no future for her village unless she confronts a distant but fast-approaching danger, and rekindles her people's long-lost spirit of seafaring adventure!

Need to know

Likes: Legends, the ocean
Dislikes: Arrogance, shipwrecks
LEGO debut: 41149 Moana's Island Adventure (2017)
Mini doll shown: 43205 Ultimate Adventure Castle (2022)

Leading role

When she becomes her island's chief, Moana wears a new voyaging outfit decorated with shells and bright red leaves.

Sequel style

Sets based on *Moana 2* feature a new Moana mini doll wearing a red woven skirt over an asymmetrical pale dress.

Ride the wave

Moana's minifigure rides an ocean-themed car in 2023's Disney 100 anniversary set Disney Celebration Train (43212).

Did you know?

Moana has also been made into a LEGO micro doll and a buildable LEGO BrickHeadz figure.

Pua

Puppyish pig

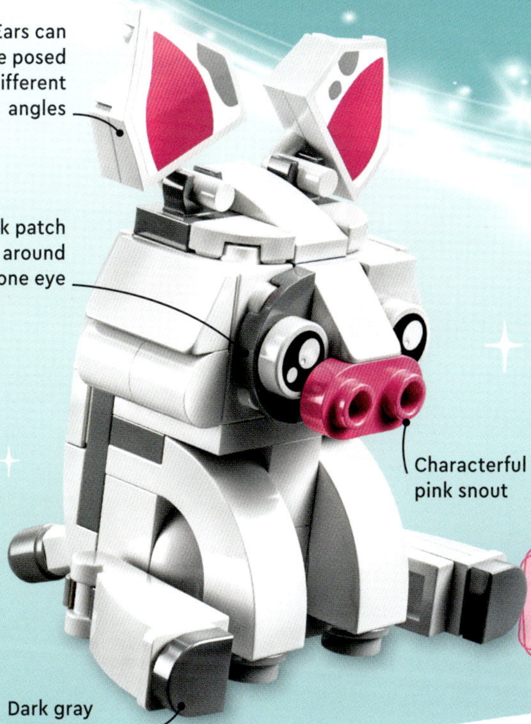

THIS PINT-SIZED PIG has been Moana's pet since she was a little girl. He senses her need to explore the ocean and joins her on her first voyage, only for it to end in shipwreck. He is relieved to see her return from her next epic journey and resolves to go with her on future adventures.

Pua and Heihei: Disney Duos (set 43226)

Did you know?

The Disney Duos set was released in 2023—part of a LEGO range celebrating Disney's 100th anniversary!

THIS SIMPLE CREATURE owes his life to Moana many times over! As a child, she kept him out of a villager's cooking pot, and when he accidentally stowed away on her ocean voyage, she saved him from drowning, from Maui, and from coconut monsters. Heihei has no idea of his debt, but then Heihei has no ideas at all!

Heihei

Checked-out chicken

Maui

Tattooed trickster

MOANA SEEKS OUT this shapeshifting demigod when her island is in danger. She finds him unfriendly, unbelievably big-headed, and unrepentant about stealing the Heart of Te Fiti more than 1,000 years ago. If she can't convince him to return the gem to its island goddess owner, the entire world will be doomed!

Need to know

Likes: Showing off, turning into an eagle
Dislikes: Losing his magical fish hook
LEGO debut: 41150 Moana's Ocean Voyage (2017)
Figure shown: 43258 Kakamora Barge (2025)

Did you know?

Maui is a LEGO "big fig"—the only one found in the LEGO Disney range and other mini doll sets.

SCENE OF THE CRIME

In Moana's Ocean Voyage (41150), Maui comes face to face with Te Fiti, who can be turned into her demon form, Te Kā!

Sina

Moana's mom

AS THE WIFE of one chief and mother to the next, Moana's mom is an important figure in her village. She is a vital bridge between father and daughter—helping each understand the other's motivations—and a strong woman in her own right. Sina wants the best for Moana, but she fears for her safety.

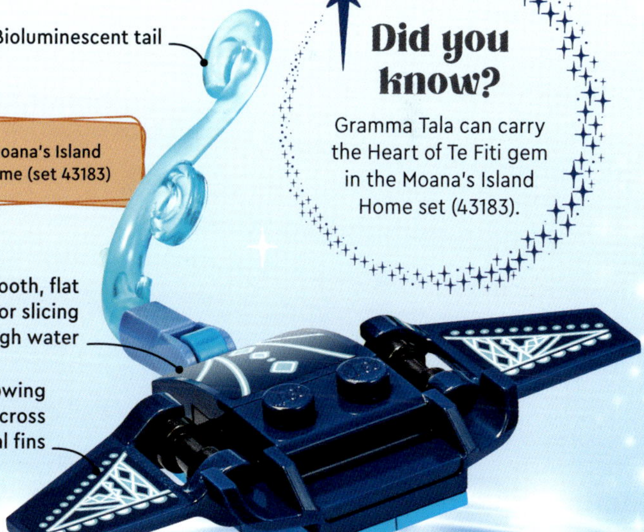

Did you know?

Gramma Tala can carry the Heart of Te Fiti gem in the Moana's Island Home set (43183).

AFTER A LONG LIFE communing with the ocean and teaching Moana about their shared history, Gramma Tala turns into a shimmering manta ray. She is never far from her granddaughter on her ocean odyssey, and when Moana needs her most, Tala resumes her human form to appear to her as a guiding spirit.

Gramma Tala

Ray of light

Moni

Making history

THIS HIGH-ENERGY HISTORIAN has spent his life learning his island's stories. Now, thanks to Moana, he gets to live an epic of his own. He is a huge admirer of Moana and Maui and is overjoyed to share an adventure with them both. Moni is also a talented crafter who likes to make Maui fan art!

Moni and Loto:
Moana's Adventure Canoe (set 43270)

Did you know?

Loto's model boat is a micro version of the set it comes in, Moana's Adventure Canoe (43270).

BRILLIANT CANOE BUILDER Loto is not afraid to fail, so long as she gets to try, try, and try again! She always aims for the best and prepares for the worst, but never stops to appreciate herself or others. It takes a voyage with Moana before she can see the value of being part of a team.

Loto

Always improving

Simea

Moana's little sis

THIS THREE-YEAR-OLD doesn't like Moana going away, but loves it when her "big sis" comes back with gifts! Simea idolizes her seafaring sibling and loves to hear her tell tales learned from their grandmother. She knows that the ocean is a friend of the family and dreams of one day going sailing with Moana.

THEY MAY LOOK like cute little coconuts, but there's nothing sweet about this husky horde. Losing their island home has turned the Kakamora into hardened pirates, surviving on a vast, ramshackle raft. The first time Moana meets them, she is lucky to escape. The second time, she is lucky to make a Kakamora friend!

Kakamora

Tough nuts to crack

Miguel Rivera

Music is his life

MUSIC IS BANNED in Miguel's household, so he teaches himself to play guitar in secret. On the Day of the Dead, he enters a talent contest and accidentally strums his way out of the Land of the Living! To get home again, he must enlist the help of his skeletal ancestors in the Land of the Dead.

Need to know

Likes: Music, the Day of the Dead
Dislikes: Family feuds
LEGO debut (shown here): 71038 Disney 100 Series (2023)

Did you know?

Miguel's dog, Dante, is a Xoloitzcuintle—an almost hairless breed that is the national dog of Mexico.

RIVERA REVEALED Miguel's collectible Minifigure comes with a second head, showing his unpainted face with a mole just above his mouth.

Ernesto de la Cruz

Music is his afterlife

THIS MEGASTAR MUSICIAN died before Miguel was born, but his songs live on to inspire the youngster. Miguel is delighted to meet his hero in the Land of the Dead, but learns he is not the idol he hoped. This skeletal celebrity stole his guitar and his famous songs—at an enormous cost!

FAMOUS FACES
The collectible Minifigure Ernesto has two smiling faces, but one is more sinister than the other!

Need to know

Likes: Fame and fortune
Dislikes: Being found out
LEGO debut (shown here): 71038 Disney 100 Series (2023)

Did you know?

The Day of the Dead is an annual holiday in Mexico to remember late friends and family members.

Raya

Guardian of the Dragon Gem

WHEN THE POWERFUL Dragon Gem is broken, it falls to this warrior princess and her dragon friend, Sisu, to retrieve its scattered parts. If they fail, a dark force will sweep their divided land, turning every last person to stone. If they succeed, the once united realm of Kumandra might just be born anew!

Did you know?

Raya's hat and hair are a single unique LEGO piece, shared with no other mini doll.

SWORD IN THE STONE
Raya defends the Dragon Gem in Raya and the Heart Palace (43181) using weapons hidden in its fold-out walls!

Need to know

Likes: Dragons, Tuk Tuk
Dislikes: Kumandra being divided
LEGO debut (shown here): 43181 Raya and the Heart Palace (2021)

Namaari

Raya's rival

AS CHILDREN, NAMAARI and Raya looked set to be friends, despite coming from rival tribes. But Namaari's desire to possess the Dragon Gem came between them and plunged the whole land of Kumandra into chaos! Years later, she is Raya's most formidable foe and no longer believes in the power of dragons.

THIS YOUNG BOAT owner teams up with Raya and Sisu when they need a quick getaway from Namaari. Usually Boun's floating restaurant doesn't go anywhere, but with a little dragon power, it becomes a speedboat! Boun stays positive in the face of sadness and danger and never gives up on his friends.

Did you know?

In a land named after dragon parts, Boun comes from Tail, Namaari from Fang, and Raya from Heart.

Boun

Boy with a boat

Sisu

Dragon in human form

FIVE HUNDRED YEARS ago, Kumandra's dragons sacrificed themselves to save the realm's human inhabitants. Only Sisudatu, the playful water dragon, remained, hidden away and convinced her noble work was done. When Raya finds her and tells her otherwise, the pair set out to save humanity all over again.

Need to know

Likes: People, honesty, swimming
Dislikes: Losing her fellow dragons
LEGO debut (shown here): 43185 Boun's Boat (2021)

DIFFERENT SCALES
Sisu reveals her true form in Raya and Sisu Dragon (43184). With her lavender hair and eyes, she is still recognizable as Raya's best friend.

Tuk Tuk

Raya's round ride

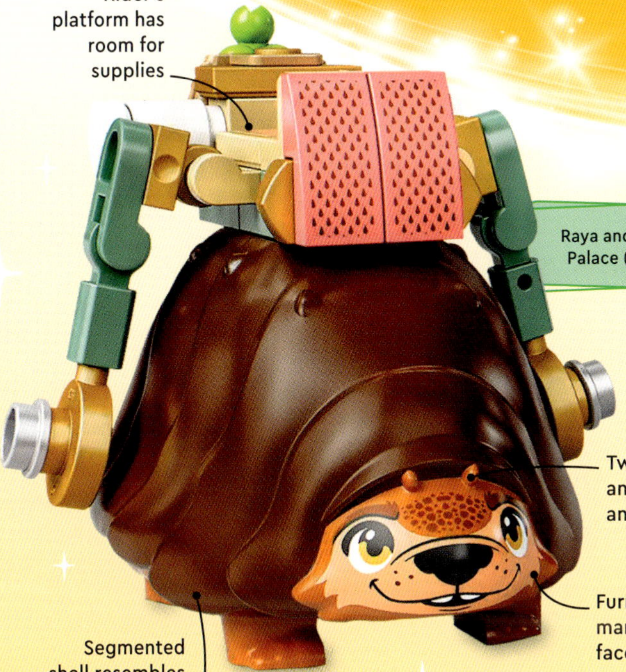

WHEN RAYA BEFRIENDED this unusual creature, he was small enough to fit in the palm of her hand. Nowadays, he is much, much bigger and serves as her main mode of transport. Tuk Tuk is loyal, reliable, and super-fast when he curls into an armored ball. Raya sits on a special saddle on his back.

THESE CUDDLY CON ARTISTS are Ongis—monkey-like hustlers that live in Kumandra's port town, Talon. They use speed, acrobatics, cunning, and cuteness to get by on their wits, until the day they try to trick Raya. She offers them the opportunity to do some good and—surprisingly—they jump at the chance!

Uka, Pan, and Dyan

Trickster trio

Mirabel Madrigal

Finding her gift

IN A FAMILY where magical gifts are the norm, Mirabel is extraordinary for having no special powers at all. But when her enchanted home starts to come apart at the seams, so does the Madrigal magic! Suddenly, Mirabel's bravery, empathy, and unconditional love for her family are the greatest gifts any household could hope for.

FAMILY GATHERING
The second LEGO version of the Madrigal family *casita* comes with Mirabel, her two sisters, her three cousins, and her grandmother, Alma.

Need to know

Likes: Her family and its *casita*
Dislikes: Not having a magical gift
LEGO debut: 43202 The Madrigal House (2021)
Mini doll shown: 43245 The Magical Madrigal House (2024)

Storybook star
Two small LEGO sets that open up like storybooks come with unique micro doll variants of Mirabel and her family.

Christmas gift
Another Mirabel micro doll variant debuted on day 20 of the 2024 LEGO Disney Advent Calendar (43253).

Alma Madrigal

Senior señora

Did you know?

Encanto is the Spanish word for "enchanting"—meaning both "delightful" and "doing magic"!

THE HEAD OF the Madrigal household is known to everyone simply as Abuela (the Spanish word for grandmother). She has run the family *casita* for half a century, respecting its magic and guiding its gifted inhabitants. But with each passing year, her responsibilities make her more controlling and fearful about the future.

Need to know

Likes: Magic, family, tradition
Dislikes: Cracks in the *casita*, talking about Bruno
LEGO debut: 43202 The Madrigal House (2021)
Mini doll shown: 43245 The Magical Madrigal House (2024)

Alternative Abuela

The first Abuela Alma mini doll came in The Madrigal House (43202), with a more confident expression and a different dress print.

Isabela Madrigal

Blooming big sister

All characters: The Magical Madrigal House (set 43245)

IT CAN'T BE easy being the golden child in an already gilded family, but Mirabel's eldest sister makes it look effortless. Flowers bloom instantly wherever she goes, yet she never trips on them. In fact, she never puts a foot wrong—unlike Mirabel, who always feels out of step!

MIRABEL AND ISABELA'S magically strong middle sister bears many burdens for her family and community. On some days, that means picking up pianos and lifting livestock. On others, it means shouldering the doubts and fears her loved ones don't want to think about. Luisa really deserves a rest, but she always refuses to take one!

Did you know?

The Magical Madrigal House set includes a donkey figure for Luisa to lift!

Luisa Madrigal

Mighty middle sister

Mirabel's Cousins

Each one given a gift

JUST LIKE HER SISTERS, Mirabel's cousins were granted magical gifts when they were five years old. Each gift suited the child's personality and came with access to a new, enchanted area of the family *casita*. Mirabel loves them all, especially Antonio, with whom she used to share her own small, unenchanted room.

Dolores Madrigal

Mirabel's eldest cousin has the gift of super-hearing. She doesn't mean to listen in on everyone's business—she simply can't help it!

Did you know?

Micro dolls feature as children in mini doll sets and as fully grown characters in smaller scale ones.

Camilo Madrigal

This born entertainer can change his shape to look like anyone. He uses his talent to amuse and to get extra servings at meal times!

Antonio Madrigal

The youngest Madrigal of all is beloved by animals. He understands everything they say and loves to ride around on a jaguar!

Bruno Madrigal

Undiscovered uncle

THE MADRIGALS DON'T talk about their missing family member—but they do like to sing about him! Listen and they'll tell you how Mirabel's uncle saw visions of the future, until an especially scary one made him leave the *casita*! His old room is now out of bounds, but could it reveal where he's been all this time?

Did you know?

Bruno is the first Madrigal to be made as a minifigure instead of as a mini doll or micro doll.

WHERE THE MAGIC HAPPENS
In the LEGO Ideas set Magic of Disney (21352), Bruno stands before a micro-scale version of the Madrigal *casita* with only a rat for company!

Need to know

Likes: Rats, magic, family meals
Dislikes: Loneliness, visions of doom
LEGO debut (shown here): 21352 Magic of Disney (2024)

Parce

Antonio's big cat buddy ...

JAGUARS AREN'T KNOWN for hanging around with humans, but this one has a magical bond with young Antonio Madrigal. The five-year-old is small enough to ride on the big cat's back, and Parce is happy for him to do so! Antonio can even understand the cat, though others hear only growls.

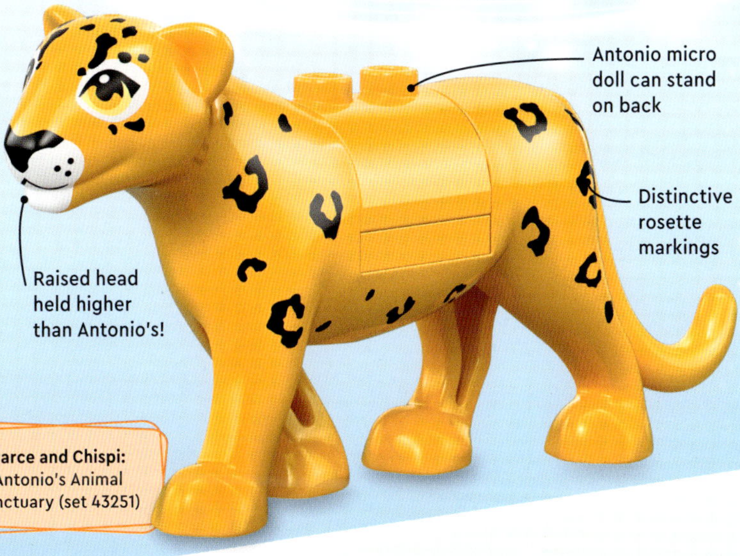

Parce and Chispi: Antonio's Animal Sanctuary (set 43251)

Did you know?

A LEGO hamster piece represented Chispi in two sets before a new figure was created just for her.

WHEN THE REST of Antonio's animal pals are going well and truly wild, this placid capybara is much more likely to be chilling. Very little moves the giant rodent—physically or emotionally—and her long, furry face seems to drip with disdain. But deep down, Chispi is as devoted to Antonio as any other creature.

Chispi

... and his capybara companion

Buzz Lightyear

A Star Command star is born

NOT TO BE CONFUSED with the toy he inspired, this Space Ranger is the real deal! He never gives up on a mission and never accepts defeat. But when his ship and crew are stranded on a hostile planet, Buzz learns that there are more ways to deal with a bad situation than simply fight against it.

Need to know

Likes: Narrating mission logs
Dislikes: Autopilots, rookies
LEGO debut (shown here): 76830 Zyclops Chase (2022)

To infinity ...

Buzz wears a test pilot's suit to fly the XL-15 Spaceship (76832), in which he hopes to achieve faster-than-light hyperspeed.

... and beyond!

In Zurg Battle (76831), Buzz deploys his famous wings and can wear hair or his classic purple astronaut's cap.

LIGHT-YEARS APART

Buzz finds his best self in conflict with the villainous Zurg, but also has to face the fact that the pair share some common history!

Izzy Hawthorne

Space Ranger of the future

Need to know

Likes: Living up to her family name
Dislikes: Her astrophobia
LEGO debut (shown here): 76830 Zyclops Chase (2022)

THIS PROUD MEMBER of the Junior Zap Patrol dreams of becoming a Space Ranger like her grandmother. The only problem is her fear of outer space! Izzy isn't scared of much else, though, and when her world is in danger, she teams up with Buzz Lightyear to save it from robots—and total erasure from time!

Totally buzzed

Izzy couldn't be happier when she finally gets her own Space Ranger gear, complete with "SR" patch on the left shoulder.

FOUR MORE EYES ONLY

When in full uniform, members of Zap Patrol (and its junior section) wear helmets that make them look like they have four glowing eyes!

Darby Steel

Not-so-junior Zap Patroller

YOU DON'T NEED to be young—or willing—to join the Junior Zap Patrol. This cantankerous old crook was given the choice of getting involved or going to prison, so she reluctantly signed up. She soon earns her place on the team, however, mostly thanks to her talent for blowing things up!

Darby Steel and Mo Morrison: XL-15 Spaceship (set 76832)

Did you know?

The distant planet where Buzz and the Junior Zap Patrol do battle with Zurg is called T'Kani Prime.

MO ISN'T REALLY SURE why he joined the Junior Zap Patrol, but then he isn't really sure about a lot of things! He has no great sense of purpose and muddles through life as best as he can. Maybe a dose of adventure with Buzz Lightyear and Izzy Hawthorne is the wake-up call he really needs.

Mo Morrison

Finding his place in space

Sox

Technical support kit

Did you know?

Lightyear is the imagined origin story for the Buzz Lightyear action figures seen in the *Toy Story* films.

Sox and ERIC: Zurg Battle (set 76831)

BUZZ LIGHTYEAR'S CAT companion is actually a robot, but he still likes having his belly rubbed! A gift to Buzz from Izzy's grandmother, Alisha, Sox is designed to provide emotional support in tricky times. And when the going gets really tough, he can also fire darts, cut through walls, and do rocket scientist–level math!

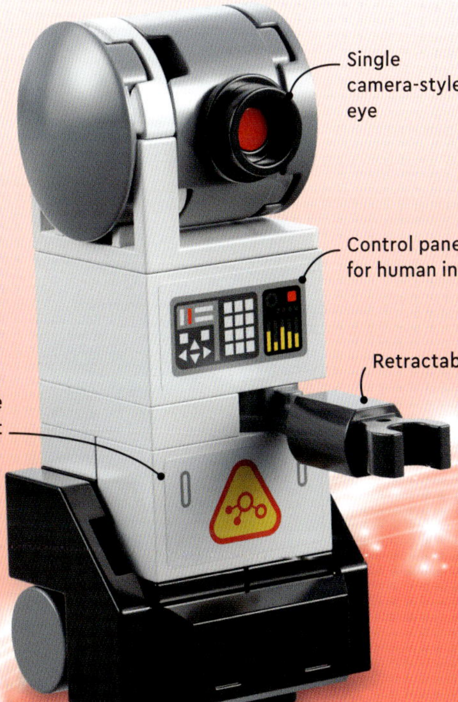

EVERYDAY ROBOTIC INDUSTRIAL COLLEAGUES (or ERICs for short) are issued by Star Command to help Space Rangers with their missions. If properly looked after, they can operate for decades; without proper maintenance, they will get a little forgetful. Know which kind you're talking to before asking for directions!

ERIC

Here to help

Asha

Rebel of Rosas

IN THE KINGDOM of Rosas, 17-year-old Asha dreams of becoming the king's apprentice and looking after the wishes he collects from his people. But when she finally meets King Magnifico, Asha starts to question his motives. She makes her own wish upon a star and begins an adventure that changes the kingdom forever!

MAGICAL HISTORY TOUR
In Asha in the City of Rosas (43223), Asha flies the flag for her magical home kingdom while working as a tour guide.

Need to know

Likes: Wishes coming true
Dislikes: Wishes being denied
LEGO debut (shown here): 43223 Asha in the City of Rosas (2023)

FAMILY AND FRIEND
In Asha's Cottage (43231), Asha can introduce her mom Sakina and her grandfather Sabino to her magical friend Star.

King Magnifico

Selfish sorcerer

THE KING OF ROSAS is a sorcerer with the power to make wishes come true. His subjects gladly give their wishes to him in the hope he will grant them, but he rarely does. Instead, King Magnifico hoards them in his castle, leaving his people with no memory of the dreams that once meant so much to them.

King Magnifico and Dahlia: King Magnifico's Castle (set 43224)

KING MAGNIFICO'S BAKER is also Asha's best friend. When Asha fears the king will never grant her grandfather's wish, Dahlia helps her free it. Then, when Magnifico denounces Asha and offers a reward for her capture, Dahlia stands firm and bravely leads a crowd of people in defying their once beloved king.

Did you know?

The King Magnifico's Castle set (43224) comes with a fully equipped kitchen for Dahlia to bake in.

Dahlia

Baking bestie

Sabino

100 years young

AT THE AGE of 18, Sabino entrusted his dearest wish to King Magnifico. Now, as he turns 100, he hopes the king might finally grant it. When his granddaughter, Asha, learns this will never happen and vows to get his wish back, it drives a wedge between the pair, before bringing them closer than ever.

Did you know?

Wish celebrates 100 years of Disney, and Sabino's age is one of the film's many nods to Disney history.

Sabino and Sakina:
Asha's Cottage
(set 43231)

LIKE EVERYONE ELSE in the Kingdom of Rosas, Asha's mom loves King Magnifico and trusts him to rule wisely and well. So the news that Asha has come to doubt the king's judgment leaves Sakina shocked and scared. But she still does all she can to help her daughter discover her true destiny.

Sakina

Mom on a mission

Star

When you wish ...

WHEN ASHA WISHES on this Star, it comes down to Earth to meet her! The glowing little bundle of joy grants wishes everywhere it goes—except in the king's castle, where Magnifico is enraged to have a magical rival. Star never speaks, but its actions tell a tale that ends happily ever after.

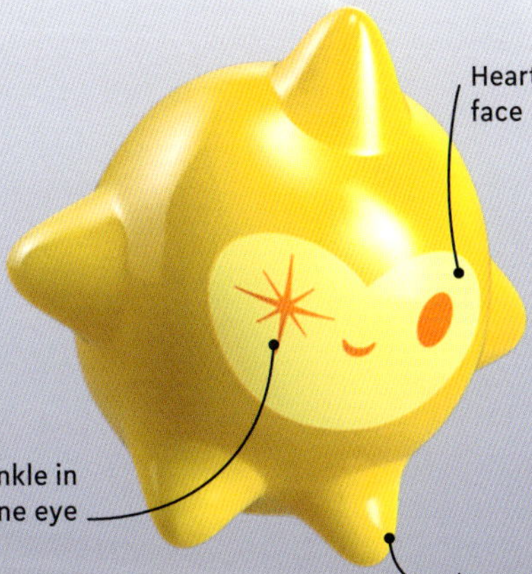

Did you know?

The LEGO Star figure comes with a transparent brick stand to make it look like it is flying.

Star and Valentino: Asha in the City of Rosas (set 43223)

MAGICAL STAR GRANTS this goat's unspoken wish, giving him the ability to talk! He may be just three weeks old, but Valentino finds he has lots to say, and a deep, dignified way of saying it. He is Asha's pet and constant companion on her adventures, always ready with a pearl of wit or wisdom.

Valentino

Wisecracking kid

Palace Pets

Furry royal friends

ALL THE DISNEY PRINCESSES love animals, and most have a pet to call their own. Sometimes, these cuddly companions even get together to have adventures without their human friends! These furry tales take place in a magical land called Whisker Haven, which can only be visited by animals and where every creature is a valued critterzen.

Treasure

Ariel's kitten is no ordinary cat, because she loves water! She met Ariel on board Prince Eric's ship, and it was love at first sight.

Daisy

Rapunzel's friends at the Snuggly Duckling pub gave her this puppy as a wedding present. Her favorite hobby is painting.

Berry

Snow White met this bashful bunny beneath a blueberry bush in the woods. She enjoys bouncing and baking cakes.

Did you know?

There are more than 30 episodes of the animated series *Whisker Haven Tales with the Palace Pets.*

Petite

Belle found this little pony on a winter's day and took her in to keep her warm. Like Belle, she's a big fan of books.

Pumpkin

Cinderella's poodle pup was a gift from the Prince. She adores balls—but only the kind with lots of dancing!

Windflower

Pocahontas is the only princess to have a pet raccoon. Windflower loves collecting things, including friends and trouble!

Dreamy

Aurora's cat takes after her owner—she's a real sleepyhead! But Dreamy always wakes up when it's time for an adventure.

DK | Penguin Random House

Project Editor Lisa Stock
Senior US Editor Kayla Dugger
Project Art Editor Jenny Edwards
Designers Molly Kellond, Samantha Richiardi
Production Editor Marc Staples
Senior Production Controller Lloyd Robertson
Managing Editor Tori Kosara
Managing Art Editors Jo Connor and Sunita Gahir
Publisher Paula Regan
Art Director Charlotte Coulais
Managing Director Mark Searle

DK would like to thank Gary Ombler for additional photography, Shari Last for editorial assistance, Julia March for proofreading, and Virien Chopra and Samrajkumar Selvasekaran for image research.

First American Edition, 2026
Published in the United States by DK Publishing,
a division of Penguin Random House LLC
1745 Broadway, 20th Floor, New York, NY 10019

Manufactured in Great Britain by Dorling Kindersley Limited
under license from the LEGO Group.

26 27 28 29 30 10 9 8 7 6 5 4 3 2 1
001–356091–Jun/2026

ISBN 979-8-2171-3983-5 (trade edition)
979-8-2173-0872-9 (library edition)

Printed and bound in China

www.dk.com
www.LEGO.com
www.disney.com

FSC www.fsc.org MIX Paper | Supporting responsible forestry FSC™ C018179

This book was made with Forest Stewardship Council™ certified paper—one small step in DK's commitment to a sustainable future.
Learn more at www.dk.com/uk/information/sustainability